FRESH BELIEFS

Keeping to Your Spiritual Path

Dear Suzan,
You have great
energy ☺

SPENCER T. KING

Spencer

BALBOA
PRESS

A DIVISION OF HAY HOUSE

Balboa Press books may be ordered through booksellers or by contacting:

Balboa Press
A Division of Hay House
1663 Liberty Drive
Bloomington, IN 47403
www.balboapress.com
1 (877) 407-4847

Print information available on the last page.

ISBN: 978-1-5043-4223-0 (sc)
ISBN: 978-1-5043-4225-4 (hc)
ISBN: 978-1-5043-4224-7 (e)

Library of Congress Control Number: 2015916351

Balboa Press rev. date: 11/13/2015

To Claudia, Annalisa, and Jimi—
Mother Earth and each of Her living souls…

Contents

PART I – WHY?

I Believe in The Magic of Life
The glory behind the veil is waiting for you.

PART II – INFUSION

Our Stories
An ending is a new beginning. The tales you tell reinforce your beliefs.

Positioning Your Soul for Emergence
Ego and fear–death by 1,000 paper cuts.

Winds of Change
"The separation is in the preparation."

PART III – TOTALITY

Notes of Gratitude

How do you thank all of the special people in your life? I have been blessed to have a tribe of wonderful friends scattered across the U.S. and in Europe, and they have all taught me the meaning of true brotherhood. In order of our initial introduction, I want to thank and acknowledge: Ken, Pat, Dale, Lance, Robert, Dwight, Mike J., Scott, Jerry, Paul, Andrew, Gerhard, Mike O., Doug M., Jed, Jeff D., Doug E., Chris, Jeff A., Randal, Thorsten, Martin, Axel, Jonas, Jason, Mike S., Randy, Uli, Cliff, Kris, Ted, Kevin, Jaime, and Rob.

To my team of initial editors: It is with the highest degree of gratitude that I give thanks and editing credit to Claudia, Ingrid, Joie, and Dwight. The four of you helped me to create this book.

To Consuelo Collier, who divinely edited and contributed to the manuscript. Thank you for your guidance and creativity.

And finally, as I state throughout the context of this book, we are ultimately our own best teachers. Each one of us, though, needs to be initially pointed in the right direction, and to consistently plunge into the deep ocean of wisdom provided to us by the world's many past and present thought leaders. This being said, those thought leaders who've been most influential to me are mentioned throughout these pages. And the teachers who guided me most profoundly at the beginning of my journey (and continues to do so daily) are Drs. Deepak Chopra and Wayne Dyer. Dr. Chopra opened my eyes by presenting to me the superlative life-plan as described in his book, *The Seven Spiritual Laws of Success*. And for this, I offer a heartfelt "thank you." Dr. Dyer's message of Divine Love delivered in "every man's voice" gives me constant guidance.

INTRODUCTION
What is Spirituality?

This thought-provoking question riddles many people's minds because the possible answers are infinite. In fact, as unique beings, we each have our own response and perception to this loaded question. For example, one person may answer by saying: "To be spiritual is to walk a life of compassion, kindness, and stillness." Yet another may respond with: "A spiritual life means to be connected to one's soul and to seek awakenings." And others may answer by saying: "I really don't know what spirituality is, I just want to make it through my day without blowing a gasket!"

Fortunately, all of the above answers are correct, because we all have our own distinct life experiences, soul lessons, and karmic contracts. And after much reflection, *my* ever-evolving response to this question is: If we are here to reach complete connectedness to each other by giving back creatively, with ultimate generosity—to mankind, the animals, the environment, and the planet—then I believe to walk a Path of spirituality is to recondition the way we *think and feel.* So ultimately, I believe we must open ourselves gracefully to be in position to...*hear God whisper to us our unique and divine purpose.*

Of course, after contemplating the above, other questions may arise, like: Do you believe in your soul? Yes? And if so, what is your genesis? In other words, do you believe your soul comes from God (or Source Energy, Spirit, the Universe, or whatever label you happen to prefer)? And if you believe you are a slice of your Creator—that your soul stems from a pure entity—do you also believe your soul, in itself, is as pure as the Source from which it stems? And if it is, can you see the sheer potential you have in allowing yourself to exist with only Love in your heart? And to thereby live only from your soul's perspective?

With all this in mind, I sometimes say to myself: *Okay, then! If I just learn to live from my soul's point of view, then I must have the ability to emanate Love at all times—which means I must also have the ability to be perpetually joyful!* But after contemplating *that* philosophy, I start to think: *Okay, but if my soul is so pure, from where does all of the gunk originate? And how can all of life's challenges and impregnating experiences permit me to live from this pure and actualized state? And if my soul—and everyone else's—is sprouted from a pure and divine source, then why do I tend to judge everything?*

What I've learned is: to live from my soul's perspective, I have to find a way to release both my grip of the past, and my anxiety around the future. And as I pointed out earlier, this requires a shift in both how I *think*, which then affects the way that I *feel*. So yes, living from the divinity of our souls, day by day, is possible. But this shift in consciousness requires a relinquishment of old outdated cognitive and emotional patterns—and I know from personal experience that this can seem like an arduous task!

Many years ago, when spirituality first situated itself into my psyche, these were some of the questions I began to ask myself. And even though these questions seemed humungous to me in the beginning, I also felt an energized anticipation and goodness around them, because I sensed a strong awakening to something I already knew. Besides, I wasn't immediately concerned with finding all the answers; I knew they would come. I also felt the innate understanding that my new spiritual journey would be a lifelong practice, so there was no need to rush to the finish line. So in the beginning, my only focus was to learn and apply these understandings in each and every day, even though I had no idea where to begin! I also knew that, once committed, I had to be sure I would keep to my Path.

So why did I write this book, you ask? Well, in a nutshell, because one like this does not yet exist. Let me put it this way: Shortly after my life's purpose was first whispered to me, I searched for a book which would fundamentally focus on "keeping me to my spiritual Path" (so I could, of course, better fulfill my purpose). And during this search, I came across many profound, well-written books, most of which had brilliant ideas and excellent spiritual content. But nowhere, in any of this material, did I locate a functional approach one could follow specifically to keep on track and on purpose, moment to moment, and day by day.

Many years ago, on the specific and miraculous day my purpose was presented to me, I felt compelled to give back to all souls by spreading this word. And that's when I decided to put pen to paper. Now, of course, the amount of spiritual content available these days is enormous, resulting in no shortage of invaluable information… and my intensive research took my thoughts and beliefs in many different directions. But in the end, I found that all spiritual roads (and research!) lead to the same destination. And it was through my studies that my new belief system began to unfold. I had no formal guide or plan laid out that I intended to follow but, as I began applying the many lessons that lie within these pages, my *intentional* life grew organically. So in an effort to help others find their way and to keep them moving forward, I designed *Fresh Beliefs* as a new approach to aid those who are on their own conscious spiritual journey, as they follow their own unique Paths.

After decades of study, I have come to realize we exist to live together in harmony. And in order to accomplish that way of life, we must all look inward and consider how to best contribute to our communities, and how to better support each other along our individual journeys. Thus, each person has their own unique Path to follow and their own specific contributions to offer.

As I've said, we all begin with a pure soul, effervescent with abundant Love, free of negative influence and fear. Over time, though, we allow life to galvanize a crust of varied layers upon us, encasing our lovely, God-given souls in dysfunctional thinking, non-serving emotional patterns, along with a whole slew of other behavioral tendencies that can greatly diminish our Quality of Life. And although there are exceptions on this planet, the overwhelming end-result is a fear-based, accumulation-oriented, status-hungry species whose lives are based on materialism, greed, addiction, control and the like.

Yet from deep within, we all have a yearning for true peace, abundance, and Love. Our journey then becomes one of asking life's deepest questions, and the realization that we all, individually, need to live from our soul's perspective so we can, therefore, collectively maximize our experience on this beautiful planet.

And if we all focused on this single concept, imagine the bliss we could create! The gifts we would receive by living an open, flexible existence would be total synchronization amongst all of Earth's living creatures. During the early days of my awakening, I learned we all have our own special gifts to offer to the world. And these gifts—when realized, harnessed, and nurtured—become our life's purpose. Remember, your purpose—your "dharma"—chooses you (you don't choose *it*, as many people believe). And to let the choosing begin, you only need to keep your heart open so you can recognize your soul's destiny when it knocks on your front door, saying, "I'm here! Let's do this!" From there, your dharma becomes your gift to mankind—and you can then give to the world your unique offerings in your own exceptional way. I believe, once we all start practicing and living from our individual purposes, humanity will be able to collectively reach our divine potential.

So to answer the earlier question, I wrote this book because I have realized my purpose. But what you probably don't know is that I once fell very hard from my spiritual Path; it was a devastating time for me. Then, one Sunday afternoon, I had an epiphany...an "awakening."

After my Sunday spiritual awakening, I decided to completely recommit to my spiritual practice—I dove deeply into the process of investing in myself so I would never again deviate from my Path. I mean, this was something I *had* to do, and I knew passion and commitment wouldn't be enough. With everything I had already been through, I knew I needed some extra help that would keep me on track and on Path—so I decided to create a progressive plan, which would serve this very purpose.

I started by developing some simple measures, which helped to keep me focused in every moment of my every day. And I like to keep my life exciting and ever-evolving, so I knew my plan needed to have plenty of flexibility. But the real key for me was to keep the momentum of my growth flowing, so I wouldn't cave during challenging moments.

And after putting my newly recommitted practice into place, I noticed some wonderful results that emerged right away! However, not until several months later did I realize the profound, cumulative effect my newfound practice was having on my life. Slowly, over time, I began to realize I was living a much more joyous, peaceful experience; I felt that, somehow, I was heading in the right direction.

You know, there is so much freedom when you live with true joy in your heart, without allowing yourself to be chained by the oppressive shackles of fear. I mean, if you think about it, you cannot have joy while tangled up in stress, pain, or anxiety...right? And by living a joyful existence, you give your soul the opportunity to emerge and express itself—you allow your essence to do what it was born to do.

I have learned there are typically two types of people that begin a conscious, spiritual journey:

1) Those who already have an understanding of their own spirituality: These folks are aware of primary spiritual concepts, and are looking to further develop their knowledge and proficiency— they are seeking some direction on how to live a consistently spiritual life. They are thirsty for more information—enthusiastic, invested, sponge-like, patient, and ready for the content to be delivered to them at the right time and in the right place.

2) Those who are less aware of their own spirituality, but know there's more to life than what they are currently experiencing: These folks are not sure what the Path is or how it should be traveled...

maybe they are even a little skeptical. They feel a need to learn more before taking the plunge. They know they need the content, but are unsure where to start or how to garner it. Yes, they are looking for answers, but perhaps from a more nervous, fearful, and/or defensive perspective.

Regardless of what category you fall into, seeking a steady, joyful life is probably highly important to you. And it may help you to know that I, too, was once facing my first steps on the spiritual Path, just as you are today. Having walked my spiritual Path for some time now, I am finally free of the stress associated with the negative emotions related to unmet desires. In other words, I no longer freak out just because certain personal goals and wants have not yet been fulfilled. And let me tell you, it took me a long time to get to this point. Today, though, I try to bring joy to every human, animal, and environmental interaction I experience. I try to bring light, a lingering smile, and certainly as much compassion and positive energy as I can muster to every experience I encounter.

So where are you on *your* spiritual journey? Are you just getting started? Or are you an experienced traveler always looking to deepen your practice? Well, regardless of your place on it, we all occasionally drift from our Path from time to time (having deviated from my own journey in the past, I understand how this can happen!). But I do know the challenge most of us face has to do with the retraining of our conditioned bundle of reflexes, especially during our most challenging moments. Therefore, determined to keep to my own Path, I developed a series of "actions," which are repeatable and, most importantly, have aided me immensely in reconditioning my own mind, so I can better control my thoughts and, therefore, my feelings as well. As a result, my ego no longer has any real success in manipulating my thoughts. *I now have total control over my mind.* I am now motivated exclusively by Love, and seek each day to live in the brilliant channel, which connects my soul to God and all that is God's loving light and abundance.

So, after renewing my spiritual commitment, and keeping more consistently to my spiritual Path, the people around me began to

As a man thinketh … so shall he be.

Mindset Matters

notice a difference in the radiance of my being. I know I was emanating a much deeper level of "calm." And sometimes a family member, friend, or colleague told me my calmer, more relaxed demeanor, along with my renewed commitment to my spiritual practices, had actually helped them through a tough time. As these comments began to mount, I thought to myself one day, *Is my purpose in life to help people keep to their spiritual Path?*

As I'm sure you can imagine, this was a huge moment for me. I mean, it's not every day you are suddenly presented with the idea of how you are going to help mankind. And I say this with the highest degree of humility and only in the theme of "doing my part." And I knew this had to truly be my divine purpose, because it felt so true, and I was immediately comfortable and at ease with the idea. So I embraced it, and spent four years developing the thought patterns, spiritual concepts, and evolutionary tools that I believe are needed to guide people who are ready for this journey. And I continue to focus on new processes every day so you, the spiritual student, will always have fresh ideas to help you Keep to Your Spiritual Path.

Great news! Keeping to my own Path hasn't required super human strength, or the loss of huge amounts of time from my day. It becomes a series of transitions from "awareness" to "shifting" to "implementation" to "growth" to "epiphanies" to "abundance" to "second-nature awareness". And I'm sure you will find that, once spirituality has taken its hold, you will better be able to open your gut—and your heart—to what's always been there, and to what's truly possible. Once you recognize this, you will innately know how spirituality works. Then it's up to you to develop, nurture, and breathe it in...*or not!* Either way, spirituality will have you engulfed in its flame of miraculous happenings and unending possibilities.

I can tell you, firsthand, that the power of God's Love has completely changed my perspective. In fact, I have never before had more direction, clarity, energy, and fun manifesting in my life. Also, I have very little stress in my day-to-day experiences. Sure, like everyone else, I will always have improvements to make and areas of spiritual development I want to further cultivate—and I look

[handwritten margin notes:] Shit happens so the 'shift' can happen ≋ · Pre-paring us to receive more! Thank you, God, for Blessing me.

forward to those opportunities! It's simply that my passion in life is to now pass on to you the information and tools I use every day for the purpose of staying on track, and keeping to the Path.

Truth: there is a one-word answer to every problem, issue, setback, obstruction, difficulty, and/or obstacle…and that answer is Love. *Love bares all Things + Covers all.*

Try asking yourself this question: What is Love? *God .*

I mean, really? What *is* Love? And from where does it stem? If you think about it, everyone has their own ideas of what Love really means, because everyone's background, conditioning, and perceptions are all so different. Have you ever truly thought about it, though? I bring this up because no one ever posed this question to me, so it wasn't until recently that I began contemplating it. And by garnering a deeper understanding of what Love is through the process of meditation, I came to the conclusion that the source of Love is God. And I know what you're thinking: *So if the source of Love is God, then what is God?*

God is pure Love. God is in me. God is my partner in creating my life experience. God is giving. God is everywhere and in everything. And if you have other notions of what God or pure Love is, that's just fine. But in the end, when you strip away all the negativity in your life, what remains? Nothing but pure spirit and pure Love. I think most of you probably understand this concept intellectually, but life really starts to fall into place once you genuinely make God and his Love the basis of your study, your application, and eventually your entire life.

Our souls come from God…it's as simple as that. And it's God's Love born into all of us that unites our souls. Yes, various cultures and ideology have sought to breed the concept of separation, but it's actually impossible to sever the authentic bond we all share. We are bound together with, by, and through Love. Where there is no darkness, there can be only light, only Love—Love for all things; Love for all people; Love for all animals; Love for the environment; and Love for one's self. To be is to Love.

I've been fortunate enough in my life to have learned from many diverse people—whether they be renowned spiritual masters and teachers, or simple "everyday" people who shared their stories of challenge and triumph. My hope, therefore, is that you will find some guidance here, while learning to apply all or some of the ideas in this book—as these are the very ideas I use each and every day, in my own life. And ultimately, only *you* can determine what philosophies, exercises, and practices work best for you. I do my best in this book to weave together ancient theories, contemporary ideas, as well as my own spiritual processes, which have helped me keep to my own Path. So my wish is that these principled beliefs help you to keep to your path as well.

Throughout the pages of this book, you will read a few stories about my life. I do this to offer some insight into my own personal life experiences so you, the reader, are aware of the challenges with which I was once faced. And the practices I developed, which helped to keep me on my Path, and ultimately helped me to rise above my own challenges, have become the book you currently hold in your hands.

In turn, I also spend time in this book discussing *emotional* fears and how to overcome them. But what about very dark fears, you may be asking, such as those involved with an abusive situation or with physical or mental illness? Well, these are complex situations, which have unique circumstances and needs, so I do not directly address them here. But I do believe, regardless of your life's situation, that we all have the ability to search for answers within ourselves so we may all find peace in our lives…and this can be highly beneficial to anyone, no matter their mental, emotional, or physical stature. This being said, minimizing the noise in your mind can offer you the opportunity to break unhealthy thought patterns, which can then open the door to more creative solutions, which you can apply in your everyday life, and with all your unique challenges and/ or circumstances. This may seem tough to accomplish if you are constantly surrounded by dire conditions, but I encourage you to give it a real go.

I strive to remain mostly neutral in my delivery, and at times I can be funny, casual, or even dorky! Occasionally, though, you may find I'm quite straightforward. But those cut-to-the-chase moments are my attempt to plow through all the sugarcoating and simply give it to you straight. In an effort to get a grip on your own emotions, you may have to retrain your mind on how to think. For that reason, some concepts in this book are reintroduced at various stages to remind you of what's most important. You'll find that certain themes pervade throughout.

You know, no one taught me how to walk down the Path. I spent years sorting through enormous amounts of information, determining how to best approach my new spiritual journey. And the results distilled themselves into the pages that follow. They are presented for you here, in order (10 "Beliefs" broken into three separate "Parts").

I call these principles "Beliefs" because, in order for you to shift into a higher state of consciousness, you must first understand *Why?* you are committed to Keeping to Your Spiritual Path. With the *Why?* comes the *Belief* in what you are trying to accomplish. And when you have a clear idea and vision of the *Why?*, your emotions subsequently energize your *Belief*, further strengthening your resolve to a point where effort becomes non-existent; your spiritual practices simply become a way of life.

You will evolve moment by moment, day by day—and you will soon find that discovery is the best part of the ride! So use whatever you garner here, and let me know what has helped you, and how you have implemented the various parts of this book into your own life. You never know…your story of how this book helped you may help someone else down the road!

Today, the aggregate of my practice has produced an emotional balance, which allows me to gracefully handle every situation that materializes. I go to the daylight at all times, regardless of what I'm facing, because that is where peace resides. Remaining positive and knowing that great things are always coming propagates a life of joy for me. I'm allowing my soul to emerge and, man, as I've discovered…that's the way to live a life!

Amen

After implementing and living the principles found here in *Fresh Beliefs*, I *desire* much, yet I feel I *have* everything.

Here is my philosophy of the Fresh Beliefs concept:

Belief One: To have all that you desire, understand and *feel* your unique Why?

Belief Two: Easily orientate your wellbeing by speaking from a healthy perspective.

Belief Three: Release your fears so you can sooner realize your dreams.

Belief Four: Position yourself for liberation and unlimited potential!

Belief Five: Allow your innate sense of curiosity to surface and to fuel your growth.

Belief Six: Nature is your constant reminder of the abundant Universe.

Belief Seven: Leverage Beliefs One through Six into secure footing on your Path.

Belief Eight: Integrate new elements into your daily, lifelong practice.

Belief Nine: Weaving it all together while co-creating your life with God.

Belief Ten: Practice and learn perpetually, serving yourself and every other soul.

Helping you Keep to Your Spiritual Path is my life's purpose—so from the bottom of my heart, thank you so much for investing in yourself! Now, let's do this together!

PART I
Why?

Our passions are driven by the sense
of freedom we seek as Creators of our
individual lives. The fuel feeding us
is the deep connection we feel to *why*
we pursue our chosen freedoms.

BELIEF ONE
I Believe in The Magic of Life
The glory behind the veil is waiting for you.

"The two most important days in your life are the day
you are born and the day you find out why."
– Mark Twain

Why do this?

Why go through an awakening process? Why choose to *consciously* travel a spiritual Path? Why go through the rigors of challenging the status quo and the "perceived" struggle of overcoming your fearful thoughts? Why unfurl your soul?

We do it because we want to be struck by something profound. We do it because we *know* the Magic of Life is ours to be had and not reserved for just the privileged few. We *believe* it is at our fingertips and it is not just some vague, transcendent dream. We embark on the journey because we want to experience our fundamental desire for full-blown freedom. ⌐ *our Destiny*

We want the mystifying questions of life to be answered. We go down this spiritual Path so we may eventually feel light and peaceful. We know there's more to life than the "daily grind." We know our brief and precious time here on Earth is for a graceful purpose, and it is not to be wasted. And we want to *feel* and *live* our purpose while we are alive and breathing *today!*

If you are the kind of person who chooses a spiritual life, you know it is an intimate solo journey, which will lead you (and those who travel with you) to a world laden with harmony and resonating goodwill. Your focus is to grow and to spread positive vibrations in all directions; to each person with whom you come in contact. *That* is why you have picked up this book. Once and for all, you want to Keep to Your Spiritual Path, and to give back to yourself and to humanity through your newly discovered life's purpose.

Most people today, though, do not believe in themselves. They feel life has pummeled them into an average existence, and they believe the steep hill before them is just too grueling to climb. And in their hopelessness and despair, they retreat from their Path, falling back into lazy, victimized, or inflexible ways of behaving. These individuals have fallen prey to the oppressive ideology, which has been permeating our planet since the dawn of time.

But all that aside, here is the real issue these people face: They fail to bridge the chasm from "want" to "belief." They can taste the dream, but cannot seem to find the "oomph" to attain it. No one, including themselves, questions their "want" to realize their goal—but to these folks "the Path" becomes a never-ending cycle of "trying" and missed opportunities, because their entire approach is doomed from the beginning.

Those who grow each day on their journey, however, take a different slant to life. They have the same dream, but move forward with the belief of *Why?* they are shifting their lives for a more abundant future. And their resolute belief in the bigger picture converts "sacrificing" into "a step closer." So one person may view "giving up something" as difficult, while the person focused on continued growth sees "giving it up" as an exciting opportunity to bring their dreams within reach.

For example, a guy who fails to bridge the chasm from "want" to "belief" may struggle more in his ability to break through his old, conditioned patterns. Let's take his drive to work, for instance. During his morning commute, he typically chooses to listen only to music, knowing he could, instead, be doing others things to further his spiritual development. In other words, his morning drive to work has always consisted of obsessively flipping back and forth between a series of radio stations, as he tries to find just the right song to ease his anxiety, and rest his weary mind. In this case, the man is using music compulsively, as a form of escape, to avoid looking at all of the "stuff" going on inside of him. He's got enough spiritual intelligence to know he could try stillness and silence in the car (e.g., being present with his breathing, his morning, and the other drivers around him). Or he could pop in the Chopra CD one of his buddies gave him the week before. However, he is unwilling to shift his investment from obsessive channel flipping to that of conscious evolution; he's afraid to make a change to the concrete way he's always done things. And therefore, his journey to enlightenment may take a lot longer. But if we look at a woman living with more spiritual awareness in her life, her morning commute looks very different. For example, she, too, listens to music on her way into work, but only for a few short minutes, to be uplifted and inspired by her favorite musical artist. She may then switch to some sort of spiritual content for the remainder of the drive. Most importantly, though, she's not afraid to be present while driving in her car; she doesn't need any obsessive external distractions that can be used as a form of escapism. She's ready and willing to look inward, and whatever she needs to face about herself, or her day, she does so calmly and courageously. Excited to learn and seek different opportunities—to apply a new lesson—the woman chooses conscious evolution over external distraction.

This book is built on the idea of converting your "want" into your *Why?* through the implementation of this new belief system. That is how you will close the chasm between "almost" and YES!

Creating your new belief system will provide a fresh perspective for your personal and spiritual growth, piety, and view of universal life. As the spawn of God, you are meant to find your way back home by regaining and living in perpetual joy. A new belief system can take the place of your current way of thinking. And this new understanding of *Why?*, and the implementation of these lively new beliefs, will break down your obstacles, while simultaneously cleansing your mind of negativity, promoting your joyous unfolding.

you are what you think about.

Only those who look within and think independently have discovered the true joy and miracles of everyday existence. The truth is, your mind takes you where you direct it. If you are nervous, fearful, or anxious, the Universe will always give you more of the same, because you have trained yourself to focus on negative energy... and what we focus on expands. *But,* what you today consider an enemy—your wicked thoughts—can be immediately converted into your greatest asset, providing you with immense joy, happiness, and peace. So simply point your thoughts in the right direction, feed them loving energy, and watch your life begin to flower. *Bloom.*

Just as the human body has the amazing ability to heal itself, the brain, too, can quickly use its capacity to help you heal your life, allowing you to live the way you'd like. So if you work, over a period of time, to condition your mind to focus on positivity, you will manifest those positive aspirations which you seek. Learn to consistently focus on good things (or the opposite of the "bad" things you are thinking) at all times. For this is how you study the art of "awareness," and how its steady application can change your life forever. Because it's actually through your awareness of your negative or non-serving thoughts that you can train yourself to think more positively.

The consciousness you acquire while strolling down your Path will awaken you to becoming more aware, grateful, compassionate, tolerant, and, most importantly, loving. These are the emotions that will compel you to continue your journey each day, allowing you to discover ever more about yourself and how the Universe functions.

But when we stand back and contemplate how we can "arrive" at such a "place," we oftentimes get in our own way. What I mean to say is, we sometimes complicate our quest by allowing our egos, outdated beliefs, and life's daily stresses to cloud the fact that discovering the answers to life's questions is really quite simple.

Did you know you can tap life's reset button at any time, instantly changing the way you feel about your existence? For example, look at your life as it is today, and realize it's your *perspective* on your situation, which, in turn, determines how you feel. On some level you *know* this. So with this knowledge, let's shed society's perpetuated and oppressive rules for good! Let's put you in a position to reclaim your deep-seated life energy, thereby allowing you to finally drive your *own* life exactly how you'd like to. The time of allowing one day to blend seamlessly into the next without living your dreams is over! It's time to liberate!

This book can give you a starting point (or, in some cases, a spiritual compass, if you will) to orientate yourself back to "true north" while walking your conscious journey. It's laid out in such a way as to breed success within you, so you can Keep to Your Spiritual Path. I believe if you know *Why?* you are on the journey, you will stay inspired to keep to it. And once you journey the Path for some time, the mega questions will naturally beg:

"Why am I here?"

Or...

"Why am I alive?"

But honestly, I believe there is too much emphasis placed on these questions. And to me, the answer is simple: You are here to realize your divine purpose; your individual dharma so your life-force—your spirit—can come forth, connecting collectively with all living things. Whether we all choose to live in a harmoniously unified fashion as a species remains to be seen, but the potential of that happening certainly exists.

You see, instead of, "Why am I here? or, "Why am I alive?" I think the question should really be: "When will my life's purpose present itself to me?" Or it could go deeper, as in: "How can I stay focused on the reconditioning process I must undergo, in order to clear my mind, allowing me to recognize my divine purpose when it presents itself to me?" *There is a plan: Jeremiah 29:11*

So what does this mean exactly? Well, asking this kind of conscious question can help you to shed your outdated, dysfunctional layers so you can live from your soul's perspective, instead of your ego's demands.

Throughout this book, I'll go over many concepts that will serve in developing your conscious awareness, so you can better recognize

In God's Perfect-time

your purpose when the season is right. For now (and as we move forward), create the image in your mind of living gently. With no agenda or attachments, gentility gives you flexibility in the moment. Keeping yourself gentle promotes a way of life that is easy, clear, relaxed, and fruitful. If you are not gentle—with yourself and with others—then, in a sense, you are "swimming against the current," often finding yourself in a state of turbulence, as you try to dodge life's boulders and logs.

Why walk this Path?

Because…it gives us the opportunity to welcome the rediscovered joy from within, and to begin to spread that joy organically. And then we can begin to feel the beautiful responsibility of passing it forward. We can begin to feel various levels of abundance flowing through us. We can give back more freely. And we learn how to invest in ourselves so we can give even more. And once we find ourselves in the flow of God's loving river, life's "little issues" no longer trip us up the way they used to…we can handle the bigger perceived problems with more creativity. We suddenly realize infinite patience is our friend, and the act of "allowing" brings more joy and goodness to us. Want a new, loving relationship? Then stop searching for someone—cease feeling lonely! Try detaching from this negative energy of searching and striving to find the right mate so you won't be "alone," and instead just live your life! In other words, *allow* that person to come to you when the season is right, instead of "trying so hard" to make it happen on your own. Trust me, this works every time. Just allow…

Imagine experiencing the life you are meant to live—giving and receiving and loving everyone, all the time. Your awakening will happen. Your epiphanies will come. You will have your enlightenment. Just listen…gently…and your dharma will eventually present itself.

Why?

Well, rather than considering what you are trying to change, let's look at an example of a life that has shifted into a higher level of awareness. In other words, let's see what it can look like if we simply allow liberating feelings to flow in and through us. *It looks like this:*

Deepak Chopra's "Sixth Spiritual Law of Success" teaches us the all-important concept of "detachment." What this means is to relinquish the attachment we have to specific results, while staying focused on the intent of achieving our desires. Then we can watch those desires begin to manifest. What does he mean by this? Well, this teaching suggests that we simply focus on the tasks at hand—on what's right in front of us—while living in the present moment, and the results we desire will eventually come. In other words, we cannot allow our perceived "lack of results" to stress us out…we cannot allow this to become our predominant line of thinking. For it is the very anxiety we feel for not having achieved our results, which, in turn, keeps them from manifesting! Yes, anxiety and attachment create limiting thoughts. For example, when I was working on this book, I didn't worry about deadlines, or how quickly I could complete it. I just wrote the words as I felt them from my heart, in each moment, one day at a time…and "poof!" a book has manifested. Focus on the moment because that's where your greatest power is…and that is the only way we can ever really feel free! There is great joy in living with freedom from negative energy. In fact, we can only manifest our desires while in that state of freedom.

Why Keep to Your Path? Because curiosity is adventurous!

Imagine a life filled with Love in all of its many and varied forms—Love can fill every nook and cranny of your existence. And you can achieve this by learning how to give and receive Love unconditionally…at all times. That's right—you have within you the capacity to spiritually Love every human and animal, in each and every day of your life. Start by stripping away your labels, your fears, and your past. The end-result, as you interact with another person, will be two human beings with no other choice but to Love one another. Imagine that kind of beauty… Is there someone in your life you miss or haven't spoken with in years because of a conflict or misunderstanding? Don't let fear, stubbornness, or pride keep you from connecting again. Maybe you have never met one of your parents. Why not give it shot? Get in your car and drive across the country to introduce yourself to the father you have never met. Who knows? It might change your life for the better!

Why not try spending some time considering a more compassionate lifestyle. Visualize what it would feel like to help that person in need, or to rescue that abandoned animal caged up at the Humane Society. Open a door for him or her with genuine benevolence. Help someone with their luggage—not just to be polite, but because you *really* want to help them. Do something special for someone today. Go the extra mile, always. Be steadfast. Instead of a quick pat on your dog's head, stop for a few minutes to really Love her up…10 times a day! How wonderful does it feel to give from the heart? Giving engenders Love. Give that which you seek and receive more of it. *L . O . V . E .*

Become consciously adventurous and curious. Expect to find treats under every rock. Do the unexpected and shake up your life in a positive way. Use this new energy to feel the real connection you have with humanity. Allow someone to pull in front of you in traffic, then feel the soulful connection with him or her. How nice does that feel? Do it all day and open your eyes to the obvious correlation we all have with each other. Walls begin to fall. The light pours in.

We choose the Path because we want the feeling of appreciation, compassion, and goodness in our lives. And when we come into alignment with that kind of universal energy, we begin to have gratitude for the smallest things. We appreciate fresh food that comes from the Earth's soil, the sun, and the people who planted the seeds, and neatly stacked the bananas. Have a greater desire to learn and become curious again. As explorers, we keep to our momentous Paths, nurturing our adventurous spirits, while searching out the mystery around the next bend. And it's that kind of curiosity that keeps us inventive and tolerant. Explore like a six-year-old again!

The spiritual Paths we walk also provide a feeling of progress, teaching us how to live in the moment, and how to string together beautiful days one after another. Imagine the feeling of going to sleep each night with a smile on your face. You are content to have a full belly and a clean bed. You drift off to sleep with your dream-life checklist playing out in your mind, as you reprogram your subconscious. Imagine that…keep at it. It's on its way; learn to incorporate infinite patience!

When you harness all of the tools and teachings available to you today, a beautiful feeling begins to come over you. Life becomes easier. Challenges suddenly aren't so difficult. Smaller disturbances that upset you in the past simply cease to exist. You find yourself handling life's biggest, most dramatic situations with more understanding and creativity. Professional athletes like to say, "The game is starting to slow down for me," as they become more experienced in their sport.

When you awaken and open yourself to eventual enlightenment, your life, too, will begin to slow down. When this occurs, you see the miracles all around you; you realize the Magic of Life. The fact that you are here on Earth—breathing, witnessing the perfection of life in physical form—is mind-boggling. And by looking at life through this pair of gracious lenses, you appreciate the simple phenomena all around you, like: a sparrow taking flight, the birth of a baby orca, or the impact a gentle smile can bestow. All of this can happen just by applying some simple fundamentals.

Why? Because the alternative is unacceptable!

So how do we determine what we want to feel? How do we know what true joy and happiness really mean? When we read books or attend workshops, we're often inspired to make changes to our lives and to apply new ideas and concepts. Then why do we fall off the wagon so quickly and so often? We deviate because, when we're challenged, we allow ourselves to withdraw to what we know to be familiar, comfortable, and what requires little to no effort for our egoic minds. I get that. So let's look a little deeper into why *you* can't seem to stay on track.

Some of you who are reading this book may feel pressure from yourself, family, friends, or society to "conform." You may be hearing things from your loved ones, like, "Who do you think you are?" or, "That will *never* work!" Or maybe you are carrying around your own internal self-defeating thought patterns, or perhaps you simply don't know how or where to begin. But this is all okay, because we are all in various stages of spiritual development, and we all have our own starting lines.

So in order to truly "arrive" at a place where making positive changes becomes second nature, consider defining what it is you want. If you want spiritual enlightenment, stop and ponder what this really means for approximately 12 minutes. For instance, perhaps you are wanting a stress-free life in which you have all the tools required to handle every situation? Put yourself in a place where you can emanate Love and gratitude for all things and, once in that space, try visualizing what this outcome might look and feel like for you. Does it seem like a long road to travel? It could be, but now is your chance to do something about it. Take action! Don't compromise your wellbeing and wallow in self-pity. Stop telling yourself "someday," and embrace what's right in front of you *now!* When you do the things you have always talked about doing, your life's desires become fulfilled. The day I began keeping the promises I made to myself, my life changed profoundly.

I contend there is no other reason for us to be here than to shed our egos and to lovingly give back at every opportunity. We arrive to enlightenment by enjoying every moment we live, by seeing the miracles and abundance surrounding us, by practicing infinite patience during trying times, and, finally, by remaining in a constant loving state. I mean, what else are you going to do with your life?

Let's keep this going by discussing a couple of important concepts, like: What is happiness? What is joy? If the goal is to live a life with a perpetual smile on our faces, how do we get there? How do we avoid deviating from the Path? The challenge is to maintain the momentum of our inner sacredness, while bursting through the immense fortification of the ego. There is no question the ego will fight back because it thrives on drama and negative energy. *A fundamental mistake we all make is to allow the conditions of our lives to dictate how we feel.*

People think they can only be truly happy once all of their external conditions are in alignment with their respective dreams and desires. But unless you shift into total awareness of your current mental and emotional state, that will never happen. Sure, you may have days or months where your life seems "perfect," but that always changes. In fact, the only constant in life *is* change. Everything in life is temporary...nothing stays the same. So allow the past to be the past. If you can begin to grasp these concepts, you will be on the right track.

Also, beware of your ego's monumental presence as you allow other people's words, opinions, and actions to affect your emotional equilibrium, wellbeing and motivations. This is how we can get our natural state of joy out of whack. And what's up with *that*? When you elevate yourself from the short-sighted drama you allow into your life, you recognize the triviality of it all. This is a major issue for many people, so we'll go into this in greater detail later on. But let me reiterate here that believing you must have happiness across the board until you can finally feel like you've "arrived" is the equivalent of waiting to be in peak physical condition without powerwalking every day. What I mean is, the quality of your exercise and diet in the moment will dictate your physical condition. And the quality of your commitment to the psychological moment will dictate your thought patterns, which will, in turn, dictate your feelings and, ultimately, your joy. You *are* your joy...it's always there. You just need to release the gunk and let your joy naturally emanate.

Why? Reality check!

Let's start with defining happiness. The definition most people follow is that happiness is based on how we feel, depending on what's going on around us—e.g., the state of our relationships; our financial independence (or the lack thereof); our physical health; the state of our career path; how many material possessions we've accumulated; etc. But if all that stuff dictates our inner state of joy, then how often are we truly happy? Constantly? No way—not under this definition, because life has a way of "happening," right? The nature of the physical plane is that an aspect or two of our lives will inevitably go sideways, resulting in emotional turbulence. So this is a perfect example of how most of us let the conditions of our lives dictate how we feel. And if we continually follow the cognitive route of "feeling bad" every time something doesn't go our way, or if we have the same cyclical negative thought patterns over and over again—for hours, days, months, or even years—our conditions will not change.

So what about *you*? Take a look at your life as it is today. Are you in the same emotional place you were two years ago? Ten years ago? Has your financial condition improved much over the years? Not at all? *Gasp!* Well, whatever you do, don't blame the economy. Don't fault the politicians or your boss. Because the truth is, *you* dictate these things. And if you wait for your life to magically line up so you can finally "be happy," and if you expect this to happen without internally shifting your beliefs, you better pack your patience, because you'll never get there.

But what about other people's actions *toward* you? Well, allow me to let you in on one of life's great secrets: Other people don't "make you" feel bad—it's *you* who allows yourself to feel those negative emotions based on what someone else says or does. Now this may be hard for you to swallow, but that's the way it works. For example, imagine someone getting angry with you for no apparent reason. Would you "respond" to this behavior? Or would you "react" to it? Because there's a difference, you know. Would you instantly become defensive and equally angry? In other words, would you "react" to the person's dysfunction, instantly mirroring back the same inappropriate behavior being expressed to you in that moment? Well, then, if that's the way you want to go, that is your choice. If that's the kind of reaction which is instinctive to you, then consider this alternative: Imagine you handled that moment with poise instead of anger, allowing it to roll off you like water on a duck's back. Or imagine you possessed the ability in that moment to calmly and intelligently speak your truth by setting a firm and necessary boundary. I mean, if you could "respond" in this way, instead of "reacting" in the *other* way, what kind of emotional state do you think you'd be able to maintain ? Once again, it's your choice.

Do something for me, will you? Go right now and literally look in the mirror (take this book with you!). Okay, now look yourself right in the eyes, and tell yourself it's your responsibility to stand up for your wellbeing by taking conscious action. Begin allowing yourself to determine how you are going to feel about every aspect of your life. Now affirm that no one else will ever again dictate how *you* are going to feel. And if you don't like what you see in that mirror, then let's go to work! Okay?

"The foolish man seeks happiness in the distance;
the wise grows it under his feet."
– James Oppenheim

Why walk a spiritual journey? Because joy is in the moment!
So how do we get there? How do we learn to live more fully in the moment? And how are we to feel happy with all of our external conditions? To begin, take a look at my definition of joy: *The perpetual feeling of inner peace and contentment regardless of outside conditions.*

Stress, anxiety, worry, and other types of fear are based on this illusionary thing called "time." Eckhart Tolle teaches us that fear needs more fear in order to survive and, therefore, fear derives its energy from time-based events. An example of a fearful time-based event is something disturbing from the past, or the fear of an event that *may* happen in the future. I emphasize "*may*" because when you realize that it also may *not* happen, you now have a stepping stone for relieving your current stressful moment. So the gist of this philosophy is that we sacrifice our joy whenever we experience a negative emotional swing, based on an event outside of the present moment. Technically, there is no time in the present moment...the "now" is absolutely "timeless," and present-moment living is how we can experience "timelessness." Or, more simply put, the moment just "is." Therefore, without time, there is no anxiety around past events, nor is there fear of a future event. And without fear and darkness, there can be only joy and light.

Consider this: If you put aside all of the external factors, which irritate or disturb you, what's left is the appreciation of being alive and of understanding abundance at all levels. And as this new seed of consciousness begins to permeate your world, you will begin to find clarity and beauty in everything and every situation. Colors will seem brighter and more intense. The oxygen you breathe will seem sweeter. The fresh-squeezed orange juice you have on a Sunday morning will be more delicious. You will begin to attract people into your life who are more loving and are living in a joyful state, as you are. Try living in the moment without the influence of time and see how your life's conditions begin to improve. Ultimately, you will realize your dreams this way...through a more present way of living and interacting. But you really have to focus on living each moment joyfully in order to become happy with your external conditions. When you live this way, negative situations minimize, and the flow of positivity opens up. You begin to attract the nicer things in life because you stop giving energy to the undesired things.

As you journey farther down your Path, you will learn to go beyond understanding spiritual concepts intellectually, and you will eventually learn how to ask for and claim what is universally yours.

To summarize: Trying to first be happy before you are truly joyful will only lead to frustration. Happiness is relative to outside conditions—joy, on the other hand, comes from within. So learn to operate with the mindset of what you *have,* instead of what you *don't have.* To lighten up your mood and your thinking, visualize a cute bunny, or your own child, or your favorite place on Earth, as often as possible throughout your day. This will keep you in a good place mentally, emotionally, and spiritually. Try remaining in that moment for a while, detached from specific results. Combine inner joy with infinite patience and experience the happiness which follows.

Truth: As human beings, we have the ability to change our lives in any way we desire. Don't dismiss this concept. Many of you understand and leverage this capability very well and you, therefore, live abundant and fruitful lives—you are realizing this truth, practicing it, and living the results! So bravo to you! Feels awesome, doesn't it? Unfortunately, the larger segment of society continues to struggle because they believe they can only live a joyous life if all of their circumstances are in order. They are conditioned bundles of reflexes, reacting to outside conditions, without first respecting their wellbeing and Quality of Life.

While walking our Path, we can eventually learn to decipher information in a split-second, and determine how we are going to feel and, subsequently, respond to any given event. I choose a peaceful state over any other option. It's taken me a long time to reach this point because there was much I had to unlearn along my Path. The process, though, is fun, because you can't deny the instant and obvious results. Somebody throws a rock at your car. How do you respond (or react?)? Again, the choice is yours...

Does Quality of Life mean peace and quiet to you? Do you want ever-lasting contentment in your life? If so, you must be willing to give up your current processes and labels. If you are easily upset or stressed out, you are not only negatively affecting yourself, but those around you. Do you realize that? Your loved ones and coworkers are the ones who have to deal with your inability to handle situations with poise, ease, and grace.

I believe putting your wellbeing ahead of anything else is paramount to your growth and to helping those around you. I know it sounds counter-intuitive to many of you because we've been raised to believe the opposite is true—as if putting ourselves last in line is a noble notion. But in fact, the opposite is true. When you put yourself last, there is little or nothing left for your own growth. Do you feel that way now? You can help yourself by investing in every moment of your life. The domino effect is compounding as the positive impact of your retrained brain and emotions reaches out in all directions to your family, pets, friends, colleagues, and into society. All of these people will grow emotionally as a result of your own growth, and in being around you. This is the true benefit of investing in yourself.

Live this approach each day while being aware of the challenges yet to arrive. Each lesson will offer you the experiences you need as you Keep to Your Spiritual Path. Soon, you will learn how the many aspects of spirituality are woven together. You will more deeply understand the co-creation process that you will experience personally with God. Transitioning to a life of joyful intention will expand your growth and your journey in all directions, leading to the wonderful life you seek. Feel the rush of discovering that there is always another level of ascension. Your journey will become one of complete happiness, leading you to the dock where your true voyage will begin, as you learn to give back with unconditional love in your unique way.

When I think of my own life, I want to eventually look back and know I made a worthy impact on those whom I touched and helped. I want to know, regardless of when I began this conscious quest, that I gave everything I had to further the evolution of humanity. But I know I must "walk the walk" *today*—in fact, I must do this in *each moment* in order to have that sweet smile cross my lips when I reflect back on my days of this precious life.

So as you read through these pages, consider your *Why?*, and what inspires you to Keep to Your Spiritual Path. Try doing as I have, and ask yourself how you want to be remembered. What is your legacy to your family and friends? Regardless of your circumstances, the way you handle them is your choice. So which way will you go? But whatever happens, keep believing in your *Why?*. I believe in you—I believe in your soul's divine right to burst through your old egoic layers, so you can begin to charge your life with joy, abundance, and passionate purpose!

Moving forward, let's talk about communicating your "storyline" and how it guides your life experiences. For example, consider the stories you tell people. Think back to the conversations you've had over the last few days. Were they full of lament, resentment, and negativity? Or were they exciting, adventurous, funny, and uplifting? Your storylines says a lot about you as a person. They also lay the groundwork for your life's direction.

PART II
Infusion

Integrating a new belief system eases the
struggle along a spiritual journey. With
one eye on restoration and the other on
Love, prepare yourself for freedom.

fly like a
Butterfly

BELIEF TWO
Our Stories

An ending is a new beginning. The tales you tell reinforce your beliefs.

Many years ago, I found myself experiencing the darkest point of my life. I had several things going on during this time: First, I had never really dealt with the emotions of losing my Dad to cancer six years prior. Also, I was going through a painful divorce from my best friend of 18 years. And financially, I was penniless. I was also getting to the point where I knew I could no longer burden my family and friends with my devastating issues. I was immersed in a dreadful soup of misery.

Finally, after a year of allowing my severe emotional swings to have their way with me, exhaustion took its toll; I knew something had to change. And it was during a long walk on one of my favorite trails that I made a simple—yet profound—decision: I knew I had to brush aside my dark cloud of despair in order to create some daylight. And I knew if I could do this, I would be able to open my mind to finding sanctuary from the turbulent storm.

Determined to end my blight and find my happiness again, I looked inward…not for strength, but for true honesty. This was the only chance I had if I was going to climb out of my depressing hole. I knew, deep down, I had to address the fact that I was being lazy and self-centered, and that I had the ability to be a much better person. You see, in order to deal with my own inner pain, I had learned how to wear a mask, which sort of half-heartedly projected my "best" side. And this emotional dishonesty was not only hurting me, but also some of the people who were very close to me. And so, ready to finally face my own inner turmoil, I wiped the steam from the mirror one day, and looked myself straight in the eyes.

Taking a hard look at my internal world was, at first, quite frightening. Initially, I paused...but I then took a step forward, deciding to finally confront the truth about myself. And you know what? It really wasn't all that bad. I already knew on some level what issues plagued me. And so, in that pivotal moment, I chose to be honest with myself, and I instantly felt liberated. By facing myself directly, I suddenly felt free of the thorn in my heel. And I bet you're thinking to yourself, *Okay, so the fruit of your new clarity was what?* Well, ultimately, I realized how selfish I had become, and how sharply I had deviated from leading a sincere life. And this moment of truth gave me the first stepping stone along my Path.

At that point, I knew I needed to find my way back to God, and to the divine purpose I was destined to fulfill upon this planet. And although I didn't know where to begin, I knew it would all somehow, someway, sort itself out. It just *had* to, right? My only anchor was the "knowing" I had in my belly; I just *knew* I would someday feel good again. But how many weeks or months would it take? Because, man, I had a lot of pain and guilt I was dealing with, so would it take *years?* But whatever happened, I knew my life would never be like it was before. And at the same time, I had this awful feeling I would forever have this hint of sadness attached to my Being. I didn't like that feeling at all, but I had no idea how to rid myself of it. I mean, was it possible to cut the cord on the gloomy weight bringing me down? I knew I needed to learn from my mistakes, and to find again that awesome feeling of leading a clean existence.

Then one day, I read a book—an *incredible* book. It became my spiritual compass and helped me to indicate my "true north." And with that newfound light—regardless of how much I might veer along my journey—I knew that, this time, I would Keep to My Spiritual Path (as long as I continued with a forward momentum through all of my "veeringness"!). And with each step I took, I eventually tracked more and more along the centerline. Over time, I started to feel much better about myself.

As I picked myself up and began again on my Path, I started to notice that when I focused on things which made me feel good… well, nice things came my way. Yes, joy feels better than sorrow. And I learned if I ever wanted to truly realize my dreams, I had to align myself with my natural state of inner joy (which is always there, inside of me, regardless!). For if I persisted to dwell on things that bothered me or were uncomfortable, I would bring more and more negativity into my existence. I understood that concept; I attract that which I am.

I make my life easier now by always doing what feels responsibly good and right. Today, that hint of sadness is not forgotten, but has morphed into an understanding of how to better live my life. My piety to my Path has led me to many "ah-ha" moments. Having been through numerous difficult challenges, I know now exactly what the search back to the Path entails. I taught myself how to find my own Path and, more crucially, how to keep to it.

Of course, I'm now years beyond that dark day, when I took that fateful walk along my morning trail, and made the decision to change my life. Since that time, I've learned how to narrow the gap between where I *was*, and where I am destined to go. In other words, I wouldn't be able to provide you with the tools to Keep to Your Spiritual Path, had I not drifted greatly myself and, subsequently, climbed back on to rediscover my own divine purpose. Because after all, experience is the best teacher, right?

So here we go…

What you have to realize is that your life experience is dictated by how you "feel," not necessarily by what you "think." Yes, your thoughts ultimately drive your emotions—but only when those thoughts crystalize into your ensuing emotions do you lay the groundwork of your tomorrow, and of your ultimate life experience here on Earth. Evolving forward down your spiritual Path will allow you to live a more free and easy life, as you shed the veils of negativity and dysfunctional, cyclical thought patterns.

Each awakening or growth spurt will propel you closer to enlightenment. When you have successfully recruited your collective awakenings to reach a higher level of consciousness, the compounding effect you feel will lead you to a greater awareness of how effortless life really is.

There are many great spiritual teachers among us—both past and present—and they offer us sage insights and philosophies as to how the Universe works. Armed with these gifts of knowledge, though, why do we continually deviate from our Paths...even when we know better?

If you are seeking a spiritual awakening, this book will position you to live from your soul's perspective, and to emanate Love at all times. Remember, the key to living the life you desire is Keeping to Your Spiritual Path. And by doing this you will learn:

- *Why?* you should keep to it
- how to define your own Path
- how to keep from deviating from it
- how to minimize and eliminate obstacles and fear
- how to ultimately live a joyous, peaceful existence

and, finally...

- how to put yourself in a position to give back to all living things

So what does it mean to grow spiritually?

Well, sometimes it's easier to define something by what it's *not*, rather than by what it *is*. And bona fide spiritual growth is not about graduating up the rungs of a ladder into a higher state of awareness. You see, achieving *true* spiritual growth is actually "horizontal" in nature. For example, if you've ever been on a long, 10-day road trip, you probably remember returning home a different person, having met many people and experiencing unique adventures. Well, your spiritual plane is similar, because graduating "upwards" implies one person being better than another (whereas we are all actually equals, oscillating in various stages of spiritual evolution). So technically, you move and grow "laterally" as you experience your epiphanies, moving forward step by step along your spiritual Path. And there is no finish line, which means you can bask in the glory of knowing there is always a higher level of joy to experience.

You will no doubt understand intellectually all of what you are about to read and digest, but is this enough? I mean, why is this book in your hands in the first place? And what are you hoping to gain from reading it? After you have invested your money, you will want to feel your purchase was worth it, correct? But in what are you really investing and, ultimately, what will you really be gaining?

Well, to begin with, you're investing your time. And by investing your time, you're saying to yourself that you're ready to shift some things in your life, and you're willing to carve a few minutes out of each day to put yourself in a position to live the life you desire. And it's this very concept that leads to what you will hopefully be gaining: You have opened your wallet so you can have this information. And hopefully this information will open your mind and your heart so you can finally become the continually loving, giving, peaceful, and abundant person you know yourself to be.

Investing in yourself spiritually is about you *giving* to yourself— and in return, I will give you a garden-shed full of tools, twine, seeds, and starter plants to help you cultivate your spiritual pea patch. You only need to provide the soil, the water, your willingness, and a steady beam of sunshine.

Visualize this:

Let's say four months have passed since you have been applying the concepts in this book. And it suddenly dawns on you that life feels so much better. Yes, you still have some "weeding" to do, but because you have tended, nurtured, and loved your garden, you now glow with the knowing that so much more is yet to come. You have *changed.* You *feel* different. You feel a warmth from within, which is opening your eyes and your heart to a *knowing* of the connection you have with God, Source, Spirit…you are realizing the connection you have with all living things. You are beginning to see the little miracles all around you. And the better you feel, the more you give to your metaphorical garden by watering and tending to it. You are excited for the tomato harvest because you can't wait to lovingly share your abundance with your family and friends, as you visualize canning your veggies and stacking them on your kitchen shelves. The sunflowers are taller and brighter than you ever thought possible. You sit peacefully in an Adirondack chair in your garden, idly just Being—knowing that, should a pest land on your basil plant, the ladybugs of non-judgment will take care of it. You are perfectly content with the work in which you have invested. You are graceful and poised. Feel the sun's warmth on your face. Allow yourself to bathe for a few moments in the glory you will feel as a result of your investment in yourself. You reap what you sow, you know, so don't rush it. Allow it to come on its own…that is why you have invested in yourself.

You now have a general view of the fruits of a spiritual practice. But what's really happening on your Path in order to get you "there"? And what will you actually be doing in the meantime? Well, here it is in a sentence:

From your first step on your spiritual journey, you will simultaneously recondition the way you think, feel, and respond, while consciously loving all things, and emanating true joy in an effort to live from your soul's perspective.

Wow! What a mouthful! You will see, though, everything will fall into place for you because you already possess the innate understanding to do this. It's just a matter of looking within at all times. And the effort you expend on your reconditioning process eventually gives way to complete enlightenment, at which time your life becomes effortless.

Imagine this: You are in a blinding snow storm. You know what home feels like, but you don't know how to return. You have lost your way. Well, allow this book to be your roadmap. Just follow the highway signs, use the railroad, ride the rivers, swerve with the detours, and even pick up the occasional breadcrumb! Stick with me, and we will find the way home together.

Reading this book will help to bring your innate spiritual understanding to the surface, allowing your conscious awareness to naturally blossom. Here you will learn how to Keep to Your Spiritual Path, as opposed to deviating from it. This is the theme of this book. Implement these simple tools and you will not wander from your Path. You may veer a little here and there, but your "awareness" will put you in position to always bring yourself back to "true north," so that, eventually, you'll never again deviate from your divine pathway.

So, you have now heard my story. But the question is, what's *your* story? Everybody has one. And what's your dream? Everybody has one.

We all envision our own unique bliss. It's like that "someday" thought running perpetually through our minds. We tell ourselves when *that* day comes, everything will be all right. How long have you had your "someday" thought?

Of course, if your story begins with a negative time in your life, but you have found a way to leverage that experience into something positive, then that's a wonderful story! Why do you think you have not yet realized your dreams? It is in large part because of the stories you tell people…and it also has a lot to do with what you are telling *yourself.* In other words, the attitude associated with your verbiage plays a monumental role in where you are in life, and where it is you are headed. The stories you tell people are a representation of your outlook on life. And when you convey the same storylines, again and again, over a long period of time, you, in turn, cement your tomorrow, both positively or negatively.

So how do you create a more positive, purpose-driven tomorrow? Well, you can start by ceasing in sharing with people the negative, "gossipy" details of your divorce, your firing, your illness, your accident, your miserable job, etc. Stop dripping negativity on people, because they don't want to hear it anymore. And if you keep telling the same glass-half-empty stories, without looking inward as to how the circumstances of your life show up to teach you, then you will never reach your dream. And if you don't change your tune in this regard, you run the risk of "settling for less," remaining marginal, while watching other folks live out the dreams you wish you could capture. So ask yourself: *Is this life and the story I tell about it good enough for me?*

Regardless of what you may believe, everyone on Earth has the God-given right to bask in the glory of passion, Love, boundless abundance, and never-ending peace. We each have the ability to visualize our own paradise. Placing any limitations on your dreams, consciously or not, will always keep you from realizing them.

It's also important to recognize that it's not necessarily your *story*, but how you *tell* your story. *"We had a great time at dinner, but it was so expensive. Had I known, we would have just stayed home and ordered a pizza!"* I mean, why deliver a diatribe over the price of the meal, thereby turning an otherwise awesome experience into a downer moment? Your friend only wants to hear about the romance of the trip and how cool it was! Remember, the listener is experiencing your moments with you, so give her the opportunity to have fun, to grow, to become curious, letting her imagination flower right along with your story...maybe picturing herself right there with you! So try this instead:

"We had a great time at dinner! The restaurant sat on a hill overlooking the vineyards. The owner visited our table and made some delicious recommendations. The filet mignon was so tender, I didn't even need a knife! It was a bit pricey, but totally worth it!"

Perspective...

Your thoughts drive your emotions. Your emotions deliver your life experiences. The Law of Attraction says you are always receiving what you feel. So keep feeling the way you do, and you will forever feel the way you do. When you learn to better manage your thoughts—and thereby your emotions—you can have a more positive impact on your today, as well as your tomorrow.

Living from your soul's perspective is to live in a state of peace. But there can be no peace when you allow the past to negatively impact your wellbeing. It's really a matter of shedding your old behaviors—those outdated "layers"—while simultaneously living with joy in your heart. This is where we are headed in this book.

If you are holding onto a negative emotion, you can simply release it. And I'm sure many of you are saying, "But the pain runs too deep—how am I supposed to just 'let it go'?" Well, let me tell you, we all have memories of being hurt, and many of us have feelings of past regret. But the reality is, we all individually determine whether we're going to hold onto the pain...or not. The good news is that we do, indeed, have the ability to let it go! I think an important part of walking the Path is to know that sometimes we can become addicted to those old painful dramas. So what we really have to do is learn how to become comfortable with what feels "good," instead of continually attracting the pain and drama to which we've grown so accustomed. If you can understand this concept, it will better help you to release what feels "bad."

Next, what is a "belief"? A belief is a thought repeated in your head, over and over again, to the point where that thought—and its accompanying emotions—begin to affect your physical reality. So to change your "belief," you must begin by changing your thoughts. And with that being said, then what is the power of "I am"? Well, if you believe and say to yourself, "I am sad," or, "I am angry," your ego will make sure you remain so. So what you're really doing with those "I am" statements is anchoring those thoughts and their accompanying emotions ever deeper into your psyche, making it more difficult to shed those dysfunctional layers. So this is the power of the "I am" label. And believe me, there is a difference between saying, "I *am* sad," versus, "I *feel* sad."

Knowing now that you can manage the way you feel by altering the way you think, try shifting from the "I *am* sad" self-identification, to the more manageable emotion of "I *feel* sad." By doing this, you now have cut the cord on that limiting, self-imposed label, and have evolved to a higher state. Now just work on letting go of the negative emotion. Keeping to Your Spiritual Path, while addressing and shedding negativity, opens up space for more positive thoughts and emotions to enter. It works every time.

A belief is a powerful emotional state of being. When you believe in yourself, you can move mountains. If you are the kind of person who wants to Keep to Your Spiritual Path, then begin believing in your ability to do so. Believe great things will happen to you every day while you wander your Path. Check in with yourself throughout each day, watching from above as your belief in Keeping to Your Path propels you forward. Banish all doubt, and allow yourself to totally believe in the process.

So what are we to do to gain that fresh air of consciousness? It's really quite easy. Take a deep breath, shake out the cobwebs, and learn to tell a different story. Stop telling your tired tales of why things are the way they are. Stop talking negatively about other people. Eleanor Roosevelt said, "Great people discuss ideas. Average people discuss events. Small minds discuss people."

Much of your life's drama may involve other individuals who occupy your space. For example, you may be putting yourself through the ringer because of what someone else said or did to you. But it's important to learn that these things are inconsequential. Ask yourself: *From where does my drama stem?* Then ponder the answer. I mean, is the source of your anxiety really worth the stress you're feeling? Help yourself by looking within, and by encircling your Being with positive energy and good people. You will soon realize you are in charge of your own thoughts, perceptions, and feelings, regardless of somebody else's behavior. This practice will attract more positive experiences into your life.

Conversely, maybe it's *you* who are bringing drama to others. If this is the case, be honest with yourself. Elevate your life experience by releasing the need to speak negatively about others. Learn to talk about the beauty of the moment or of tomorrow's dreams. Live from your soul's perspective and know compassionate understanding and flexibility toward other people's opinions provides the peace you seek.

Telling a different story can start with being grateful for the little things in life. For instance, be joyful you have the ability to open your eyes in the morning. Give thanks that you have a bed in which to sleep. Consider the miracle of how your lungs function by pulling in life-sustaining oxygen. Walk outside and appreciate the fresh air.

Living from this perspective is an amazingly easy and a healthy first step on your spiritual Path.

Learn to tell a new story in which you *believe,* and watch tomorrow immediately show signs of improvement, adventure, and exploration. Rediscover the infinite possibilities of curiosity. Allow yourself to feel light and sprite again. It's within you...let it out! Since you create your reality according to how you think and feel, and according to how you give back to all living things, do yourself (and everyone around you) a favor—you owe it to yourself. Consider what you *have* in this life, not what you *don't* have. Even in your darkest moments, the simplest mantra of, "This, too, shall pass" (Corinthians 10:12) can change your perception and take the edge off. And this will allow you to move toward joy.

Your "new" story begins with a shift in perception. We will go deeper into "shifting" later on. But for now, consider the things that make you happy. Is it your pet or your favorite sports team? Perhaps it's spotting a bald eagle soaring overhead while being in Nature? Or maybe it's making passionate Love to your partner in the middle of the afternoon? Whatever it is that gets your juices pumping, just begin focusing on these things that delight you. Maybe it's the thought of living in a different neighborhood, or a glass of cold sweet tea while sitting under your favorite tree on a steamy day. Contemplate a very nice existence, and knit together a story about the special things and dreams you want to create in your life. Allow the goodness you are now creating to permeate and flow through you. Tell yourself a new story of accomplishment and horizon. Do this over and over and over and over and over. Use only positive thoughts and words to weave together your new reality, or to enhance your existing one.

Walk your Path in positivity and watch blissfully as the river of codswallop spewing to you now turns into clear, crisp ambrosia. Abundance is yours to be had; I invite you to create your new story now.

But we need a starting line!

If you want to evolve spiritually, it helps to understand where you are "now." And taking an "emotional inventory" will do just that for you.

You must know by now that nothing in your life will change unless you invest in yourself. Sorry, but there's no magic pill which will vault you into instant peace. You can't just wish for things to change, all the while refusing to grow internally, and expect new and better results to immediately appear. If you want peace in your life, you can only find it within, by practicing Love at all times. If you want Love in your life, you have to invest in yourself in order for that to become the predominant aura of who you are, and who you want to be. You have to allow your soul—your spirit—to come forth. Your soul is patiently waiting, you just need an opening. As you allow your true self to come forward, the feeling of weightlessness and abundance will be ever-present, as if to say, "I've always been here! Now let's *do* this thing!" But if you say you are too busy to meditate, or don't have enough time to read or practice, then you will always be "too busy," and forever stuck in the quagmire of unrealized potential. Don't be that person.

Throughout this book, I'm going to ask you to try some things. I call these exercises "stepping stones" because, well…we're on a "Path," right? And each stepping stone is an opportunity for you to try something new, or to apply an already-heard-of concept with a brand-new perception.

Here is your first **STEPPING STONE**:

Imagine you are watching yourself from above, floating 20 feet overhead. Now try observing yourself from this angle as a total stranger. Watch how you feel and generally react to life's circumstances throughout a typical day. What do you see? Are you watching a happy, balanced person? Or are you seeing someone looking more like a victim of circumstances? Be honest in your assessment. Spend a few minutes disseminating the person you see. Also, as you continue to watch yourself, are you judging people? Are you approachable? And if you had the opportunity to do so, what aspects would you change about your personality? More importantly, what are your feelings about the various facets of behavior you just observed in yourself?

Now, while viewing yourself from this vantage point, which emotional energy would you inject into yourself, that might better help you to fulfill your dreams? For instance, would you inject more calmness? Emotional equilibrium? Or perhaps you might infuse more confidence? And what impact might this new energy have on you and your overall lifestyle?

Now assume it is two weeks later, after you have injected these new "energy characteristics" into your very Being. In other words, now that you've spent a couple of weeks acting from a calmer, more confident demeanor, now how do you look? But the big question is: How does the new level of joy you are experiencing make you, the observer, feel? Do you feel relief? Love? Well, if you feel happy for yourself, this is an indicator you are ready to enter your Path with the injection of *intent*. Because it's with intent and awareness that you will be better able to progress down your Path.

I know this stepping stone can be difficult to experience. However, when you allow yourself to realize there is tremendous potential in your "Beingness," you will approach your new self-investment not with false hope, but with energy, enthusiasm, and a knowing you are here for a greater purpose. And it is this understanding which will drive you to innately strive moment by moment toward honoring the deep peace within you. It is your instinct to be peaceful, to be loving, that will fuel you forward to each subsequent stepping stone along your divine pathway. But if you are denying this truth, that's simply your ego and your intellectual Self talking...and that's okay. When your ego takes command, though, it is in those moments that it becomes a little more convenient to resist this truth.

So when denial is present, the aggregate of your current emotional inventory is doing the talking (as opposed to the sacred, highest part of yourself). And these two "components"—the ego and the intellectual Self—are actually your "opponents," because they are keeping you from your peace. Why? How? Because your ego represents your fears, and your intellectual Self represents the imbalanced thoughts that can wreak havoc on your emotions. And these "opponents" must be recognized so you know what it is you are trying to move beyond. You can accomplish this by peeling away the old conditioning and unhealthy teachings of your past experiences. And once you learn how to shed those unhealthy layers, your inner peace, grace, and poise can emanate to those around you, spreading your loving aura like magic dust touching everyone.

Next, I want you to contemplate the questions below. I want you to spend some time really considering the feelings that emerge when you read these questions. My intent with these questions is to help jumpstart you in taking an emotional inventory, which is something you must do before beginning this journey. Once again, honesty is critical:

- Am I doing anything to improve my emotional state in every moment of every day?
- Am I willing to shift my thinking and try some new ideas and techniques?
- Am I willing to take some new steps in order to feel better?
- Am I willing to address the deeper issues of my life?
- Do titles, material things, and labels dictate my happiness?
- Do I have the same self-defeating, cyclical thoughts every day?
- How long have I had these imbalanced thoughts?
- What surface issues am I dealing with?
- How honest am I being with myself?
- How do I feel most of the time?
- Do I want to feel differently?
- How open to new ideas am I?
- How am I at handling stress?
- Am I fearful of change?
- Am I on a joyous track?
- Am I okay with change?
- Do I love myself?
- Why not now?
- Why not me?

Now trying making an honest assessment of your responses to these important questions...this will give you a good starting point. We will not address each question individually here, but I will ask them again at the end of the book in a slightly different way—this will allow you to compare your newfound feelings with your outlook on life. It's important to continue to inventory yourself over a period of time, in order to see where you stand, and how you are growing and changing as you traverse your own unique Path. As you move farther and farther down your Path, your need to take emotional inventories will decrease, because walking a healthy, spiritual life will become second nature to you.

Investing in yourself is how you make the world a better place!

Eventually, those stories you tell to yourself (and others) will innately shift to stories of positivity, openness, and understanding. Soon you'll start to notice that you're talking with others about abundance and how wonderful life is. You will also become fearless and, best of all, when the time is right, your dharma—your purpose—will present itself to you. And eventually your positive impact will be felt by someone else who needs to be inspired to find their own way along the Path. The global momentum is here now! There is a societal transformation happening on this planet, a paradigm shift of elevated consciousness, an awareness enjoyed by millions of people who realize the enlightened Path is the only way. Even conventional television programming is starting to offer more spiritual content—social media is also helping to spread the word and, when you listen closely to people, you will hear spiritual content either directly from them, or more subtly in their undertones.

You have the opportunity now to become part of this grand shift. Have you ever considered why older people are the wisest among us? It's because they've come to a realization in their existence of what's most important in life. So don't wait any longer—accelerate your learning curve this very moment!

Now let me ask you this: How were you initially introduced into the world of spirituality? After all, you are reading this book with the hope you will find "inspiration" (which stems from the phrasing to be "in-Spirit"), and to begin laying the groundwork to help you Keep to Your Spiritual Path. So where do we begin? How about with *my* story! So here we go:

I first started learning about spirituality over a several-year period. It all began when my Mom gave me Deepak Chopra's *Seven Spiritual Laws of Success* in January of 1997. I was mildly interested, so I cracked it open with no real idea of its contents. Sure, I knew Deepak was some kind of a spiritual guru, but I was otherwise unfamiliar with his teachings. *Manifestation? Pure Potentiality? Detachment?* What the heck does all of this mean? So, not willing to "get it," I closed the book, and my mind, to Deepak's teachings (which is actually okay, because I wasn't yet ready for those *kind* of teachings). At that point in time, I was still in my "spiritual womb," so to speak. So I put the book back on the shelf...for 14 years.

Time passed, and I went through my life like most people do; just trying to make the most of my days. Working hard, paying my bills, and having some fun when I could. During this period in my life, I was married, and had a thriving business. I traveled a little bit here and there, and had some cool hobbies. I guess you could say that, generally, I was quite happy. And it was during this time, in 2011, that my Mom (thank you!) introduced me to the phenomenon of Rhonda Byrne's movie, *The Secret*. She said to me, "This is awesome!" Well, I have to tell you that the teachings in *The Secret* hit me like a ton of bricks! I watched the movie dozens of times, taking its messages of positive and abundant thinking with me into the world.

From there, I started reading every Law of Attraction book I could get my hands on, such as: *You Can Heal Your Life*, by Louise Hay, and *The Power of Deliberate Intent,* by Esther and Jerry Hicks. I found my best reading and/or "absorbing" time to be at night, right before I went to bed. My Mom always taught me to go to sleep smiling, so I would read, read, read, sleep well, and begin my next day with a healthy perspective. And I began a more conscious practice of living positively and really was feeling good about myself and my life. Then it happened...

One night while I was reading, I felt as though, "Wow! I really get this! Now I know what to do." Then, I smiled and closed the book...for the last time. I decided I didn't need to read about the Law of Attraction anymore. I didn't need to watch *The Secret* anymore. That's right—I naively decided I didn't need to practice anymore.

After I made that fateful decision, what do you think became of my life? Well, as I'm sure you have probably surmised, things began to unravel...to fall apart. To begin with, I started making selfish decisions, which greatly contributed to the disintegration of my happy marriage. I also came up against financial obstacles, which forced me to sell my business. All in all, I was experiencing the most challenging time of my life. And in experiencing these very dark moments, I wasn't really sure which way was up. Fortunately, I had a wonderful support structure of family and friends who helped me through it all. However, it was my daily (and sometimes *twice* daily) walks in the woods, which acted as my true savior. And it was during many of these walks when I realized we truly are our own best teachers.

About a mile from my house is a trailhead that leads into the forest. On many days, I would walk this trail, simultaneously processing my life, while appreciating the beauty of Nature all around me. I've always had a deep, profound connection to all things in the natural world. I'd been walking this particular trail for about 15 years, and I knew whatever troubles or challenges I was facing at the time, could be sorted out amongst the mountains, trees, rivers, and wildlife. (Did you know that gazing upon a single flower in a vase can have the same effect?)

This trail I walked, over and over again, also allowed me to talk out loud to myself during these difficult days. For me, voicing my thoughts while alone in the wilderness is a wonderful way to work through my emotions. One Sunday afternoon after such a walk, I returned home with a strong and curious urge to, once again, pick up Deepak's book. And so I sat on my couch and read *The Seven Spiritual Laws of Success*, cover to cover, in about 87 minutes. When I read the last word, I took a deep breath, closed the book, and smiled. "Now I truly understand this!"

Although totally unprepared, I was deeply awakened in that moment. Deepak's presentation of the "Spiritual Laws" had an unexpected impact on me. It was as if a shroud or veil had been lifted from my psyche, exposing the previously mysterious workings of the Universe to me. I don't mean to say I understood the complete and complex balance of the Universe in that very instant, but I did feel its perfection, as well as its embrace. Also, my awareness of myself and my own behavioral patterns became acute. I suddenly felt light as a feather because, in that instant, I knew all of my "issues" were self-imposed. All the drama in my life—the "stuff" I was battling each day, and the associated negativity around it—all seemed suddenly so resolvable through Love, learning, and liberation.

My next (and practically simultaneous) thought was equally impactful: *I will not deviate from this Path again!* And in that moment, I was 100 percent sure I was going to establish a program for myself, which would prevent me from straying, or letting my "taskmaster ego" (thank you, Dr. Dyer!) get the better of me.

Initially, I had no idea what my new "program" might look like. In fact, I didn't even look at it as a "program." I just knew I was going to have to live a more conscious life, and to be more aware of my own behaviors and thought patterns. But it was all so exciting! Now I know what Dorothy must have felt like when her world switched from black and white into brilliant technicolor! Follow the yellow brick...*Path*! Ha ha!

From there, as the days and months passed, I became a sponge for all things spiritual and philosophical. I purchased books, CDs, and DVDs. I watched spiritual programing whenever I could (thank you PBS and Oprah!), and I finally began to meditate. I even set alarms on my phone, which reminded me of the spiritual concepts by which I wanted to live. And almost if by magic, people with similar beliefs, on a similar Path, began to filter into my life. I began to feel very good about my direction. I was actively applying many of the lessons I was learning. The overwhelming amount of philosophical information that is available these days became mind-boggling—but in the end, the concepts and ideas resonating within me began to trickle down to what felt right…and what worked specifically for me.

Simmer down now!

Ultimately, each one of us is trying to find ways to recondition ourselves so we can live a God-conscious life; to realize we are all "Love-emanators," and we are all connected and part of a great Source.

So in your quest to positively recondition your own self, you have to sample many different techniques and ideas in order to do so. More importantly, you then have to appraise the results and determine which of these new ideas will help you along your own Path. We all have our own unique experiences, starting points, and belief systems. What works for me may not necessarily work for you. But the creative juices that flow through you as you learn to "slow your mind," so you can absorb all of the beautiful teachings that come your way, will begin to reduce down to a practice that works very well for you. I call it your "Spiritual Layer Cake." But the question is, what will *your* Spiritual Layer Cake look like? (More on this later!)

As many of you know, we go through a transformation after experiencing very difficult times. In my case, I lost some special relationships that may never be restored. Of course, I wish only Love for these people, and hope they, too, are once again healthy and smiling. But it really is how we handle ourselves after we go through those challenging times, and how deeply we look within for growth, when we begin to make sense out of the grand journey on which we travel.

I do have to say that my spiritual development would not be as evolved as it is today if it weren't for the relationship I have with Claudia. She, along with her daughter, Annalisa, and her son, Jimi, have opened their hearts and given me a brand of Love I never before knew existed. Claudia's fire and compassion astonishes and challenges me every day. Annalisa, a young and thriving teenager, constantly compels me to bend my mind creatively. And Jimi, a newly minted seven-year-old, reminds me how easy it is to return to laughter when I allow myself to do so.

Yes, I am here to say that my story changed from one of painful divorce, financial ruin, and having to sell my business, to one of possibilities, adventures, generosity, and being peaceful. Ultimately, I learned how to recognize and harness my dharma. And it all started with a willingness to tell a new story, by moving forward with joy in my heart.

And now I look forward to hearing *your* new story!

If it makes sense and feels right to tread on your first stepping stone of spirituality, then you may have some things to overcome. You may be skeptical. And you may have significant fears, which are blocking your acceptance of new ideas. Or worse yet, you may be so blinded by those suffocating, outdated layers, that you don't recognize the damage you're causing to your own life experience. You may think you are just fine when, in fact, you are more off-base than anyone else in your life. So turn the page to read about the fearful thought patterns, which may be keeping you from the life you are destined to live.

BELIEF THREE
Positioning Your Soul for Emergence

Ego and fear—death by 1,000 paper cuts.

"Not all those who wander are lost."
— *J.R.R. Tolkien*

"How am I going to make it to payday?"
"He's going to get upset if I tell him."
"I can't because it hurts too much."
"I'm mad for what she did to me."
"I'm tired of being controlled."
"I hope I don't see him there."
"It's never worked before."
"I hate my job."
"I'm so lonely."
"I can't do it."

Do any of these thoughts sound familiar to you? It's dreadful to live with these feelings day after day after day. Have you ever thought about the sacrifice you are making to your Quality of Life by repeating these negative mantras time and time again? You are on perilous footing with these lines of thinking; you are literally designing your tomorrow with the harmful thoughts you think today. If you want your life to change, only *you* can change it! Unearthing those non-serving patterns of thought, and learning how to completely retrain your mind, may sound like a difficult thing to do—but I *believe* in you, and I know you can shake your fears. And I *believe* you can walk away from those fears because I have done it myself. I *know* you have it within you to elevate your new life experience by detaching emotionally from the things which haunt you.

I *believe* this because you are your soul. Recognize this understanding. To authentically acknowledge yourself is to identify with the purity that exists deep inside of you. And your true essence—your soul—fears nothing. So as you start to play with the idea of shaking those fears from your very Being, understand that doing so involves only a slight shift in perspective. You are a beautiful person. *Allow your full potential to step out of the shadows so it can face the sunshine again!*

Your fears and your conditioned way of thinking may make what I'm about to say difficult to swallow, and some of the philosophies in this book may be challenging for you to fully understand...so stay with me here. This section on tackling your fears is really the most important portion in the book, so pay close attention. Yes, you can bask in the glory of positive thinking and apply every awesome lesson you've ever learned to live a more glorious, purpose-driven life—but until you checkmate your fears, you will not have the opportunity to blossom into your full potential within this lifetime. Do you get that? If not, read that sentence again (and again!) until it resonates with you.

Quashing your fears is a process. It can take time, but you are not alone. As you Keep to Your Spiritual Path, you will gain a vibrancy and level of joy, which can buffer the sting of fear. And the longer you Keep to Your Path, the easier it is to remain plugged into this conscious way of life. Ultimately, it's your constant awareness of your partnership with your Creator, which allows you to live without any fear-related issues.

So far, I've talked a lot about the beautiful gift of perspective in this book (and I will continue to do so!). And when you choose to use this tool of stepping outside your own conditioned box, you give yourself the opportunity to feel out how things may look when viewed from different vantage points. And this can work as a valuable asset in your life, because this exercise allows you to better do your "homework" prior to making an important life decision. Observing life's so-called "challenges" from different angles offers you the possibility of trying different approaches, until you eventually find the one that fits best. In other words, if you're in the habit of assessing life's "situations" through a fearful or anxiety-ridden viewpoint, try stepping back and looking at the challenge from more relaxed and creative angles. And then, if you happen to discover a positive, nice-feeling solution, which stems from your newfound "shift in perspective," wouldn't it make sense to further research this creative solution, and perhaps pursue it?

Remember, you have the ability and the knowledge to approach everything in life from the angle of your choosing. And when you shift your viewpoint around an issue that typically causes you fear, you are then able to cast a new light in that particular issue's direction. From this vista, you are then in a position to minimize or eliminate the fear associated with the issue.

Homework completed, does your previously fearful viewpoint continue to make sense for you to experience? Probably not. Having delved deeply into what the other side feels like, you've now done the work to prepare yourself for plunging into a better-feeling perspective. It's much easier to just jump into the cold water and just do it, than to feel the water slowly creep up your legs and belly, which only serves to drag out the drama.

So rather than being fearful of facing your anxieties, look at it as a fresh opportunity to claim the joy, which is already yours. Darkness has lived within you for far too long; your ability to step into the light is simple because the daylight has never left you (it's just had to put up with a bad neighbor for a while!). So gently, but with conviction, determine that you are ready to claim the "You" that you know yourself to be!

As you face each issue in your life that you've dreaded dealing with, the energy you've previously dedicated to your negative emotions will probably be looking for a new home. So why not channel this energy immediately into the power of positive thinking, and do so *without any apologies!* Just let the joy pour out of your soul from its deepest place. Let it squirt out of you in all directions. Scream and laugh out loud for as long as you can! Allow the total free-flow of joy to spill out like it never has before.

Check this out:

> "Tell me, what is it you plan to do with
> your one wild and precious life?"
> – Mary Oliver

I mean, WOW! Have you ever read a more profound, direct, and challenging sentence than *that?* Try reading it again and really absorbing it. Now, *there* is motivation to tell a new story!

But it's time to get into the nitty-gritty.

Now we're going to spend some time *addressing* fear. Because in order for you to truly move forward, you have to be able to digest the idea that you can only have the life you desire when you move beyond your mind-based fears.

I understand there may be fears you are not yet ready to address, and that's okay. At some point, though, you should stop "thinking" about the life you want and begin taking some "action," so you can have the life you are meant to live! This is the only way you will be able to move beyond your fears and swiftly into a healthy, joyous state. And if you are able to simply "consider" releasing your fears—in the name of your own wellbeing—then we will have made some progress. I am inviting you to come along on this journey to a better way of living. And while you Keep to Your Path, you will find many of your fears will go away on their own accord. Your ability to introduce constant positive energy into your life will assist you in releasing the fears which plague you today.

As a human being, you have two choices in life: You can either choose a "spiritual" path, or a "material" path. The former teaches you to live with compassion and love, while the latter teaches you about accomplishment, accumulation, greed, and rivalry. One path leads to enlightenment and peace, the other is driven by fear. So which Path have you chosen? If you are not sure, ask yourself this question: *Do I allow fear to dictate my decision-making process? Well, what's your answer?*

Of course, our goal is to live a spiritual life while being surrounded by the things we enjoy. But it is the motivation driving us to possess those material things, which determines how and why we make the choices we do.

If you remain locked into the idea that fear is part of your fabric, then go back and re-read "Part I." Because remember, it's important for you to understand *Why?* you are reading this book. And when you are ready to proceed with a flexible mind (as in, "I guess I can be open to hearing about some of these new concepts..."), then you can move forward to the next phase of *believing* you can eventually rid yourself of darkness.

Let's get real!

Understand something: *It is time to kick your fears to the curb!* They have had their way with you for far too long. They have not contributed to your Quality of Life in any way, shape, or form. In fact, the opposite is true. Here's the deal: Your fears are driven by your ego. Your ego knows its survival is contingent upon providing you with a never-ending pipeline of superbly crafted, veiled untruths. So let's banish the ego's illusionary fear-based foundation once and for all. Yes, that's right—I am going to help you slay your ego...death by 1,000 paper cuts!

Try this on for size:

The elimination of fear means to simply *do* the things you fear doing, and *face* the things you fear facing. Because when you do and face the things you fear, then those things no longer have paralyzing power over you. For example, do you have a fear of heights? Then, baby, you better go get a ladder! Then, on Day One, step on the first rung and hang out for a minute or two. On Day Two, yes, step safely to the second rung. And on each new day, safely take another step higher. Use caution when doing this so you don't fall! You get my point. The longer you practice this, the less fearful you will be. What about speaking in public? Is this one of your major fears? Then, baby, you better go get a microphone! Or how about joining one of those speaking organizations (like "Toastmasters," for example), so you can surround yourself with other like-minded people who want to overcome their public-speaking fears, too! Like you, everyone in the group will have very little speaking experience, and this can make you feel a little more at ease in challenging this fear. Learn and speak so you ultimately become confident and fearless!

Moving on... the odds are your fear is much greater than the effort it will take to rid yourself of it. Fear is created in your mind, not from the authenticity of your heart. Once you have accepted this concept, you are a big step closer to removing the fear from your existence. Now let's take a stab at a simple idea that can put a new spin on your view of your fears.

STEPPING STONE: Let's have a little fun with fear! Remember, anxiety, dread, panic, stress, etc., all come from the ego. And since I, personally, don't want those kind of emotions in my energy field, I've learned to see all things fearful in a completely different light. The ego thrives efficiently because it operates by its own fear-based rules. And "rules" spelled backwards is "selur". Sounds kinda sinister, doesn't it? And since I give the negative aspects of the ego no energy or respect, I will, from this point forward, be calling the ego "selur" (lowercase intended!).

You see, "selur" likes to prey on you because it knows you have a tendency of allowing your thoughts to run quickly and effortlessly into the vast darkness of fear-based emotions. As such, your life may have become a day-by-day cycle of unrealized dreams, fueled by anxiety-ridden behaviors. Let me ask you this: Do you have the same dreams today you had 10 years ago? If so, it's in large part because you have no control over the chain of thoughts you have regarding a particular set of worries.

As far as my own worries, they have always been financial, as in: *Will I have enough money to pay the power bill?* On many occasions, I'd be having a wonderful time, hanging out with friends, enjoying their company when, suddenly, the thought would creep in: *How will I make payroll this month?* Then my mind would run through a sequence of anxious thoughts, my stomach would flip-flop, and my joy would completely disintegrate.

And what do these "worries" or "negative fantasies" look like, you ask? Well, for me, personally, I would imagine having to tell my staff their checks will probably be short (or that I wouldn't be able to give them their paychecks at all!). Then I'd think about how it would affect my business and, ultimately, my reputation as a professional if word somehow got out that I couldn't pay my staff. Long story short, I was allowing my fearful thoughts (about ridiculous things that would probably never happen!) to totally control how I felt—I allowed these thought patterns to get the better of me. And because my non-serving thoughts were cyclical in nature, I set myself up to actually have these dire circumstances occur in my life! *Oh, brother!* Does this ever happen to you?

So then we combat our negative thoughts by trying to think positively, right? Well, I am a strong advocate for the idea that you can't simply "think positively" (without doing any of the deep, internal reflection), and expect your dreams to just magically come true. Yes, you certainly can manifest anything you want by *feeling positive.* But unless you address your fears, along with the source of your own inner turmoil, then those fears and that turmoil will continue to exist (even on a lower level). And this will keep you from experiencing the life you are meant to live and enjoy. And who wants *that?* Not me, brutha!

Dr. Chopra defines "responsibility" as: "The ability to respond to a situation." He reminds us that it is up to us to decide how we are going to feel about our external conditions. As I notated earlier, nobody can "make" you feel bad; you are the one who actually "decides" to feel bad based on your life's conditions, or because of what someone else has said or done to you. Dr. Chopra also brilliantly states that, if you don't begin to shift or change out of this way of living and/or thinking: "You become the victim of your past, and your tormentor today is yourself left over from yesterday." Wow! How is *that* for a truth!?

"Flick of the Switch!" (Thank you, Angus Young!)

Regardless of the emotional investment you have in your fears, you must find a way to step out of yourself to understand how weak "selur," your ego, really is. This is a critical area in your emotional development as you Keep to Your Spiritual Path. But instead of addressing your fears and taking on the arduous task of moving through them, first you must realize that fear is rooted in darkness. Consider this: What happens when you shine a light in a dark room? The darkness disappears! So just imagine fear melting away like hot water over ice. How cool is *that!?*

But what if you can't find the light switch? Have you ever found yourself in a metaphorical dark room, feeling and searching the walls for that elusive switch, desperate to flick it? You can feel the bulb so you know the light is there. In this moment, what do you do? Well, don't fall victim to what's comfortable by simply stuffing your pain, as you would normally do. Remember, your life can change TODAY! And right now, in this moment, you can take your life in your own hands! Begin thinking about increasing your overall wellbeing, heightening your awareness, and thinking about this book you are reading as an incredible learning opportunity.

Realizing you are about to experience growth by facing your fears is to finally recognize the daylight within. And it's in this precise moment of recognition that you will find, and flick, that switch... vaporizing fear's grip on you. And the switch will begin to present itself more often as this becomes second nature to you. So get ready... because you have another new truth: Fear equals daylight for you from this point forward! Fear equals opportunity for you from this point forward! Let yourself be around and open to your fears more often so you get comfortable with facing and dealing with them on a regular basis. Just as we learned earlier, facing the issues in our lives that cause us fear, and doing so with more courage and calm, all boils down to a shift in perception, as far as our vantage point *regarding* those fearful situations. So try looking at fear as a way to broaden and deepen your spiritual growth. Seek out all of your fears and shine the light right on them. Facing and eventually releasing your fears creates a massive, sudden void within your Being, which can be instantaneously filled with the rush of joy and unlimited potential.

But what does "shining a light" really mean? Well, after the darkness (fear) disappears, you now have the opportunity to simply deal with your situation(s) with a clear, calm mind, which is now full of creative solutions. In other words, the situation may still remain, but your negative emotional attachment to the condition is gone— and this gives you the ability to access a healthier perspective, in which you can assess your situation from a totally new angle, while determining the best move forward. And when you hear it stated as such, the pressure releases a bit, doesn't it? Again, how cool is *that!?*

Okay, so let's get back to how you can actually "shine the light"? First, remember what I wrote earlier, that fear is time-based—it thrives on the resentment of your past, and the anxiety you have about the future. Think about that for a moment: If a past experience is still haunting you on this day, in this moment, that means you have not yet learned from that experience. Because if you *had* learned something from that past experience, you would be living this moment with much more creativity and peace.

Critically, you are wasting massive amounts of energy if you are worried about tomorrow, and what *could* happen "if" or "when." But when you release the fear of "what might happen," you can experience a jolt of energy unlike anything you've ever imagined. This happened to me one time, during one of my long walks, while I was just Being in Nature. Without even thinking about it, I was able to let go of a significant fear I was having—and it happened completely on its own. It was like I could feel the fear being pulled from me, roots and all, as it just kind of slid out of my body. It left me with a split-second of emptiness. "What just happened?!" I asked myself aloud. And before I could answer, the void the fear left was immediately filled with a rush of energetic joy! Arms reaching toward the sky, I exalted and felt as if I could jump over Mount Si! This rebirth for me resulted in a domino effect, as I watched all of my other fears evaporate over a period of just a few months. Today, I fear nothing; everything is as it should be.

I fear God!

Fair Warning: Imagine if the void you create by releasing your fears is not filled with Love, but rather with more fear? Suddenly the idea of releasing the old muck and mire doesn't seem so great anymore, does it? Don't be one of those people who replaces one fear with another. If you pulled a thorn from your finger, you wouldn't jam it back into your heel, would you? I hope not! When you have released a fear, it's critical you allow Love to fill that empty space.

Coming up are some exercises that will help you to eliminate your fears. As you consider these options, imagine what your life might feel like if your fears were banished from your existence. Where would you direct all of the energy your fears used to consume? Imagine the possibilities of being able to experience the simple pleasure that is your birthright: *just Being!* Just Being peaceful. Just seeing how bright the colors really are. Realizing God is everywhere, including inside of *you*. God's energy is within you. You are in partnership with God, co-creating your life. And if you learn how to embrace this truth, you can obtain access to total, utter, complete abundance…in every area of your life! It is yours to be had! Keep to Your Spiritual Path, and soon this will all begin to make sense to you. Pretty remarkable, huh?

You already are an expert at manifesting, but you most likely practice this subconsciously. But when you Keep to Your Path without deviating, you can learn to manifest with real intent. Then you can bring into your life experience anything you want. This requires nothing more than total awareness. Stick with me on this. It will eventually come to you…

In "Belief Four," we'll discuss in great detail how to prepare yourself for a successful journey on your spiritual Path. But for the specific upcoming exercises, I want you to prepare yourself emotionally prior to pulling the thorn of fear.

When you are ready to face those fears of yours, first make sure you're in a groovy state of mind. Yes, you will be facing your fears, but don't let this intimidate you. Just remember your fears come from your thoughts…they're not real! Try going back to the feeling you previously created of living a fearless life. Let this peaceful state of Being soak in, and make this positive emotional state your life's priority. You need only to think positively—I mean *really* positively—about something…anything. Once you find that "something positive" to focus on, you will be asked to face a significant fear in your life, and then to release said fear. When you do this, the void left behind will be immediate. In the moment this happens, you will first feel exhilarating relief unlike anything you have ever experienced. But just to make sure another fear doesn't eventually creep into that voided space, be sure to fill it instantly with that "something positive" you prepared ahead of time. Truly fill that vast hole with as much Love as you possibly can, giving "selur" no opportunity for re-entry.

When Love has taken the place of the void, spend the next moments focused on the rush of a new life! Your possibilities will feel vast! It's important now to move forward in your days with "conscious awareness" because "selur" will not stop trying to re-enter your psyche. So use your newfound positive energy to keep "selur" at bay. But don't worry…soon the day will come when the cleverness of the ego has no chance against the Love and purpose you have created in your new and abundant life.

The great basketball coach, John Wooden, spoke often of "rising up to a challenge." He believed when you embrace a difficult moment—whether you do so emotionally, mentally, or physically—you set yourself up for success. Victory then is evermore sweet! Well, I believe overcoming your fears can be met with the same approach. When you possess a verve-filled attitude while taking on a fear, you will burst through that wall and celebrate a new dawn, a new day, and a new life!

As the exercises approach, you may want to come back and read this section again as a reminder of how to prep yourself. So here we go…

Two fear factors:

Now for a word or two regarding strength. First and foremost, you don't need strength to overcome anything in your life. Basically, "needing strength" implies you are battling against an undesired emotion. And if you must rely on strength to deal with that which is undesired, your battle will persist forevermore, even on the faintest of levels. See, whenever you go against the natural flow of things, you will encounter resistance. You, as a rocky shoreline, will eventually be broken down by the crashing waves of fear. And when you employ strength, you are giving too much focus on this kind of negative energy.

You have been conditioned by society to be emotionally "strong" while trying to overcome your fears, but I don't believe this is the healthiest method to attract freedom into your life. Not a single measure of strength has been expended during my travels along my spiritual Path, because my approach has been one of curiosity, Love, fun, and infinite patience. A total buy-in of this concept engenders an overall feeling of, "I'm okay, and everything is working out." Over time, this mantra morphs into, "I feel great, and I know something awesome will happen today!"

When you focus on Love to move through your perceived issues, your energy flows in a positive direction, and you end up landing in the arena of creation. So instead of constantly reaching for "strength," my advice is to consistently tap into the discipline of *awareness*—this will help you to train yourself in shifting away from stress and anxiety, and into Love and imagination. You can then develop more of a deliberate intention concerning your thoughts and their accompanying emotions...and this will cannonball you into the infinite ocean of possibilities through the creative partnership that can only be relished with God.

I'm now going to address two topics with which many of you struggle: the inability to forgive, and harboring limiting beliefs. These two topics are driven fiercely by "selur," and will halt or stagnate your flow of abundance, unless you dive into these issues and take care of business!

As you read the following information, no doubt your own unresolved issues will rise to the surface. If you are the kind of person who values emotional freedom, you must keep an open mind to the prospect of releasing your inability to forgive, as well as any limiting beliefs you may be harboring. I believe your freedom is very close at hand, so please read through the following material carefully.

Forgiveness: If you are harboring resentment toward yourself, or toward someone else from your past or present life, you are doing yourself more harm than you may realize. Of course, it is perfectly natural if you feel guilty for a wrong you have done to someone, or if you feel victimized for a wrong done to you. But when not properly dealt with over long periods of time, regrets tend to abound, breeding themselves into full-blown rage and antipathy.

Resentments creates stress...it's as simple as that. And stress is a common denominator in almost every physically manifested illness. Stress and resentment work like a poison, slowly killing the human body. And quite frankly, stress is the antithesis of our ultimate goal: peace, quiet, joy, purpose, and Love. Therefore, the resentment you have chosen to lock into your psyche is extremely detrimental to every level of your wellbeing, and will keep you from making real progress as you journey along your Path.

I was once in a position in my life of having to ask for forgiveness. In trying to overcome hurting someone supremely close to me, I tried to first earn forgiveness by conducting myself the way I should have from the beginning. Over time, I thought I had proven myself worthy of having regained the trust I had so foolishly broken beforehand. So finally, I felt compelled to ask for the forgiveness I thought I had rightfully earned and deserved. At the time, though, I didn't really know what forgiveness meant, other than allowing myself and the other person involved to move forward with our relationship, unencumbered, no longer carrying the burden of what my past selfish actions had created.

But on the day I asked for the forgiveness, I wished I'd had a better idea of what it—"forgiveness"—really meant. I didn't realize then that the person giving real forgiveness would experience true liberation from carrying that burden. I would have asked for it differently had I known how. By holding onto the pain of the past, you cannot move on. You can work through a very painful, lengthy process and finally let the wound heal, leaving a scar, but it will always be there as a reminder. And that reminder will remain, making it difficult for the relationship to once again flourish. In fact, it can lead to the end of a relationship, as it did in my case. I had a hard time forgiving myself for what I had done. I was living in the past with it all.

Your other choice is to actually *give* heartfelt forgiveness, which doesn't mean you're letting yourself or the other person off the hook, but simply releasing the deep pain which you both carry. This will leave you feeling liberated, clean, and alive. But more importantly, forgiveness puts you in a position to live with joy in your heart.

When you truly forgive and release the pain of your or someone else's past actions, you free your mind of tortured thoughts, creating an open space for a new life full of dreams and joy to emerge. You are free now to tell a new story. Through forgiveness, your entire existence can change in an instant.

Getting back to the person I hurt earlier in my life...well, I carried the burden of my actions for two years. No matter how hard I tried to move on, it wasn't until I forgave *myself* that my life changed completely, and I was able to finally move forward.

Giving forgiveness to someone does not have to be a long process. Do you have a lot of your emotions invested in the pain of the past? Did something that someone else did to you hurt so bad you can't even *contemplate* forgiveness? Well, I get that. But whether it happened five years ago or five minutes ago, ask yourself how much longer you are willing to carry the pain. It's not a badge of honor to have "been strong and now I'm over it." Unless you have forgiven that person or yourself, you will always carry a piece of that past trauma with you...and this will inhibit you from moving forward, and attracting new relationships that carry with them a higher level of consciousness.

Some people have such a low self-esteem that they hold onto the pain of the past, in an effort to keep a piece of that person with them at all times. But wouldn't it be better to release the pain, and then allow the occasional smile to cross your face when you think of the good times experienced with that person? Do you want to live a free and joyous life? Or are you just that comfortable with misery? When you were born into your body in this lifetime, I doubt you said to yourself, "I want misery, and I want it to last a long time!"

If you blame your misery 100 percent on someone else, it is time you try a new approach. Regardless of how you arrived at your situation, you somehow played a role in creating the pain associated with the situation—be that role large or small. When you take accountability and responsibility for your actions (however slight they may have been), a branch is then extended to you from the "Cliff of the Victimized." And from that terrifying rock, you can then reach for the branch and pull yourself up to "Liberation Point." When you begin to grasp the fact that your joy is not in the hands of someone else, you will be able to walk away from that cliff and never look back. You only need to be willing to grasp the branch and pull yourself up, and joy is yours to be had. This is an empowering moment for you... so give yourself a pat on the back!

A side note: Just as your misery cannot be 100 percent blamed on anyone else, you also cannot expect a person to give you 100 percent of the joy you seek. That, too, must come from you!

Stepping Stone: You have probably told yourself for so long it will be impossible to forgive. But if you truly want to be free, decide forgiveness will now be simple and inevitable. Part of your new belief system is to change your view on forgiveness. Today we create a new belief. Remember, a belief is just a thought repeated. Now start telling yourself over and over that forgiving will be simple. Make up your mind that the heavy weight hanging painfully in your heart can be easily lifted and set aside.

Now simply open your mind, stand up for your wellbeing, drop the victim label, take a deep breath, and say out loud, "With all of my Being, I forgive and release the burden I've been carrying—be gone with it!" Now step back and look at it. Let it go and be free. When you can do this, you will truly step away from the negative energy field, which has encapsulated you for so long. Give all that past resentment a glance over your shoulder and say with conviction, "Goodbye...we are no longer together." And then watch all of that negative energy simply evaporate. (Be sure to complete this exercise or the burden may return.)

Now go forth, tell your new story, and regain your joy. Or as it's been said: "Change your thoughts, change your life." (Thank you, Wayne Dyer!)

Limiting Thoughts: We all have them. And the truth is, limiting thoughts will keep you from realizing your desires. Not providing forgiveness is an example of a limiting thought pattern. Here are some more examples:

I'm too busy/I don't have enough time.
I'm not smart or experienced enough.
I've always done it this way.
I can't/won't change.
I could never do that.
I don't trust people.
Nobody loves me.
I weigh too much.
I'm not attractive.
It costs too much.
I hate myself.
I'm too lazy.
I'm too old.

If you live your life with these types of thoughts rolling around in your head, and you repeat them to yourself day after day, month after month, and year after year, you are stuck in a pretty wicked cycle. It's time to take a hard look at the limiting thought patterns swirling around inside your head—for if you do not begin to shift away from these kind of unhealthy cognitive patterns, then these negative results will show up in your future. Is this what you want? Remember...*thoughts are things!*

Or perhaps you might like to finally lead a joyous life? Then drop the negativity! Forget about the conditioned, subconscious comfort you have with it. Contrary to your ego's efforts, life is not out to get you. As I've already discussed, it is you who allows negativity to impact your Being…or not. You can begin to address your limiting thought patterns by not hanging out with naysayers (or at least begin changing your tune when you're around them, and maybe the naysayers will follow suit). If you truly want sustained joy and happiness, then you have to learn how to tell new, fun, and more joyous stories! Talk about your future as something bright and cheerful.

Honestly speaking, you can't move on until you address your issues. And to properly address that which is holding you back, I highly recommend a method that has been around for years, and is now gaining real notoriety. It's called Emotional Freedom Techniques (or "EFT," for short). Nick Ortner wrote a book based on the EFT phenomenon called, *The Tapping Solution*. Borrowing from ancient acupressure techniques, he describes in simple terms how addressing deep-rooted or surface life issues, while simultaneously tapping on various parts of your body, can reduce or eliminate that issue.

It's astonishing how simple and easy tapping is for people. Nick points out that you cannot move on to a completely joyous life unless you release your pains and limiting beliefs. I agree with him. All of the positive thinking in the world is not enough. Only when you feel clean and start living from your soul's perspective can you then begin to live with complete peace in your life.

In the end, the best way to rid yourself of limiting thoughts and beliefs is to give no attention or energy to them. Simply focus on the opposite side of the fence. You say, "Sure, Spence—that's easier said than done!" Ah, busted! That's a limiting thought! Let me offer you an example of how to focus on the "other side of the fence": Instead of reeling from the thought of going to your crappy job each morning, be happy you actually have gainful employment, and begin looking for a new and better job with this new perspective. It's always much better to look for a new gig while you're already employed, right? You receive what you emit.

Stand up for your wellbeing!

Believe it or not, fear is the chief reason why people deviate from their Path. They allow themselves to fall off the wagon because it's easier to do what's comfortable for the ego. The very sad fact is that many people are more comfortable with their pain than they are with the idea of changing a few things in their lives to achieve joy. Yet when you fall, you beat yourself up. But falling is actually okay. You have permission. It's going to happen. We're all human and we're all in the process of uncoiling generations of misdirected training.

In this moment of metaphorically falling, though, just give someone a smile and get right back on your Path. Don't make a big deal out of "taking a step back." If that happens, so what!? You are in the process of changing how you live your entire life. You are investing in yourself. This is a transition period for you, so you will have some setbacks along the way. But no matter what happens, pick yourself up, dust yourself off, and Keep to Your Spiritual Path.

So how do we best handle perceived obstacles and challenges? Well, as I've been saying, it all boils down to a shift in perspective. I'm simply asking you to give yourself a break. The very fact you are practicing something new is enough to allow yourself to feel good about yourself! It takes the pressure off. You may not always see instant results, but know all of your efforts are paying off on a subconscious level. The fruits will come!

Just start by accepting that you may have some challenges along the way. You must allow yourself to be vulnerable and trust the process and the true investment you are making in yourself.

STEPPING STONE: Here is something you can do to offset limiting beliefs, and continue in your quest to transcend fear and anxiety: When you experience a fear-based moment, remain aware of how you are feeling. When fear (in any of its forms) is "triggered," immediately elevate your awareness. Allow your awareness to remind you of "selur's" manipulative intentions. Remember, when fear and anxiety surface, it is not your soul that is talking; it is "selur" trying to deliver its usual dose of terror in order to keep your spirit suppressed. Its potion is looking for the pathways into your mind, which it has been controlling since your birth ("selur" feels very cozy there).

The fear "selur" has always produced needs more juice to keep it thriving, but here's the irony: "selur" is actually more fearful of you than you will ever be of it! It knows that once you see past its camouflage, you can put a sudden end to its existence. Just put your foot down and say, "I stand up for my wellbeing!" Now smile and shine the light, and "selur" will eventually dissolve into the wretched corners from whence it came. Be gone, "selur"!

In fact, as Eckhart Tolle teaches us in *A New Earth*: *"...many people will have outgrown the ego by the time they reach their early 20s. Ego will be recognized as no more than immaturity associated with childhood and adolescence."*

Wow! Can you imagine *that*?! Consider how a consciously aware society can cease in providing fertile ground for the ego. And since more children are being raised today with the idea of living in the present moment, there will come a point when the time-based existence of the ego no longer influences our lives. So why wait? Why wait for that time to come when you can tame and ultimately eliminate "selur" altogether today?

End your fear-based life by just applying some more daylight. In fact, from this point forward, anytime you are met with stress or anxiety, I want you to focus on the concept of *daylight*. So from now on, fear equals daylight. Think "daylight" and shine the light of opportunity onto the moment. Look for the daylight, no matter how subtle it is, in every issue, during each moment. *Understand every irritant or issue is an opportunity to learn something new.* When the quality of your awareness is high, your search for daylight supersedes the stress you would otherwise feel.

Remember, every "negative" situation you experience is a chance for you to grow, regardless of what's happening around you. In the darkest moments, there is always daylight somewhere. Practice awareness by saying to yourself, "Okay, this is a real drag, but what am I going to learn from this? It's so hard to even conceive of anything positive right now, but I know this, too, shall pass, and I will be a much wiser person because of it. Maybe I can be the example of calm consciousness that everyone needs in this situation right now..."

This type of internal dialogue will help you immensely. In fact, if you are in a place where you can speak out loud, do it. The key is to be aware of how you feel and then to point your thoughts in a positive direction so you can "feel" your way to a better place.

Below is what I do when faced with a challenging moment:

As soon as I feel negative energy coming toward me, I take a deep breath and say to myself:

"Okay, everything is as it should be. Stay aware. Don't knee-jerk react. Take in the information. Stay cool. Breathe deep. Listen, listen, listen. I value my peace of mind. I know how to stay creative. Listen, listen. Stay cool. How can I best help this person? Focus on creative solutions and let them evolve. Feel peaceful. Smile from the inside out. I feel myself growing. I feel the building block being laid. Now, gently respond..."

Those are the kind of thoughts I allow to run through my mind, and sometimes I even say them aloud to myself. And this type of positive self-talk keeps me from compulsively reacting during a challenging moment. Remember, snap judgments fueled by fear can lead to regrets later on, or to the heightening of an already bad situation. Keeping my mind focused on the state of my overall wellbeing leads to more creative solutions. This is all part of the reconditioning process that you are now starting to undergo.

Now let's talk about labels...

As you begin to live each moment fearlessly, be aware of the pitfalls...because "selur" has woven an intricate tapestry of labels by which you have learned to identify yourself. Identifying with labels is a cunning and subtle tactic "selur" employs. The labels you carry around your neck have become your burden and will be one of the first areas of your life you must target for evaporation. What I mean is, do you believe you are a "parent" or a "mailman" or an "athlete" or an "attorney" or a "writer"? As you begin to awaken, you will learn you are actually none of these things. These labels are simply tags for activities you execute during this lifetime.

Don't you see, your Quality of Life has become contingent on how well or how poorly you perform under your label identifications.

And you have been taught to base your wellbeing on that subsequent performance.

Doesn't that sound dangerous? More importantly, as you begin to really grasp this concept...doesn't this *feel* dangerous? Now, step out of yourself for a moment and look at your life...evaluate how much stress you carry day in and day out, relating directly to the labels you have been conditioned to place on yourself. Eye-opening, isn't it?

That's right—"selur" has you believing you are a "mom" or a "boss" or a "teacher" or a "barista"—a "divorcee" or a "cancer victim" or a "basket case" or a "homeless person." And since the majority of the un-awakened populous believes in these kinds of labels, the cycle is perpetual. But in actuality, you are a pure soul full of Love, light, and abundance. So learn to drop the heavy importance you place on your labels (and the fears associated with them), and begin living from your soul's perspective.

Dr. Chopra's "Sixth Spiritual Law" teaches us of detachment from results. So let go of your attachment to what you are not receiving and feel your anxiety melt away. Your soul knows only joy and Love...so *give* joy and Love. Live with joy in your heart. Allow your spirit to be the predominant force in your life. Let it emanate and watch your Quality of Life increase as you build real purposeful momentum, moment by beautiful moment.

Look at it like this: Your fears and limiting thoughts act like blind spots when you drive your car. So if you don't look over your shoulder, and double-check your side-view mirrors, you will probably crash. Eliminate the blind spots in your life by opening your eyes to the amazing world in which you live. Recognize the little things that are working in your life, like making the green lights while in traffic, or having access to clean, fresh water anytime you want it. These simple acts of gratitude and awareness allow the energy you would otherwise give to your fears to be used more positively and constructively. Allow yourself the freedom of living a life focused on the good things, large and small.

Absorb the idea that life has many teachers, and as you learn to become more aware of this from moment to moment, you will find yourself living a more content life. As you Keep to Your Spiritual Path, you really will begin to see and feel your progress. You'll begin to handle things much better. And each situation you bravely soar right through becomes like a building block for you. The wasted energy you once gave away to fear and anxiety is now a positive, gurgling, energetic source. Like a mountain spring, it's always available to you, dedicated to becoming a calming influence on you and those around you. Allow yourself the potential to feel excellent in every breath you take.

You can do this! Be who you are. Be your soul, not your labels. Be Love. Walk your Path, fearlessly!

So now you have learned fear is something you can overcome through the use of awareness. You may feel inspired now to take action but, before we get ahead of ourselves, let's make sure you are set up for success. After all, this process is not a "get rich quick" scheme, nor is it a "drop 18 pounds in one week only to gain it back" ploy. The following "Belief" will help you enter your period of transition with a head start. This transitional time is critical for you, because it may seem like you will be constantly battling your tired and entrenched thoughts. But by breathing new life into your awareness, and continuing to create your new belief system, you will soon see and feel real change in your life. You will succeed!

BELIEF FOUR
Winds of Change

"The separation is in the preparation."
– Russell Wilson

As a spiritual student, you are most likely to stagger during the challenging transition from "who you are today" to "who you want to become tomorrow."

Keeping to Your Spiritual Path is like anything else you have *tried* to change in your life. Whether it be losing weight, re-budgeting your income, or repairing an important relationship, stepping foot on your new Path is much the same in that it's a new discipline for you—a new challenge—and one to which you must commit and stay dedicated.

This being said, do you ever ask yourself why you have not persevered? Why it is you begin your journey inspired, but after a week or two you resort right back to your old cyclical way of thinking and marginal performance?

"I have to wait for the right time."
"I don't know where to begin."
"I tried, but it was too hard."
"I don't have the energy."
"I will start on Monday."

How many times have you said the last one? Me, too. Funny…

But it's in the spirit of supporting your transition, of helping you Keep to Your Spiritual Path, that I have written this book.

I promise you that you have it within you now to be whoever you want to be!

You and I are going to put you in position to bring your divine purpose to the surface—and we're going to do it together! So if you wonder why you can't seem to let go of the difficult emotions that have been holding you back, you will learn here how to release those. And if you question why you snap at people for the smallest of reasons, I can help you with that issue, too. If you contemplate why you redline with such frequency, I will also give you some ideas on how to solve that little problem. And if you are just plain tired of judging other people and conditions, I will show you how to be acutely aware of your surroundings, so you can release that turbulent, damaging practice and live a more compassionate life.

Transcending the prior issues all comes down to one simple understanding: *you create your own reality.* You bring conditions to your life by the choices you make moment to moment. And I know this Law of Attraction principle rings true, because I live it every day. And when it eventually clicks with *you*, you will be forever changed. That is what conscious awareness will do for you. And once you "get it," regardless of how you choose to live your life, you will know and witness that you truly are creating your own reality. From there, it's up to you to determine how you will travel through your life, and how you will traverse your own Path. Most people, though, are in their spiritual infancy, so they are unaware of this Law—they haven't yet realized the power they truly possess to manifest their own circumstances. What about you? Are you aware of it? Well, you are now!

You see, your soul lives a spiritual life regardless of your beliefs in how you think life unfolds. The Universe responds to you by providing the chain of events you are requesting—and thereby "attracting"—through your thoughts and feelings (whether you are aware of them or not). Knowing this, you can now choose to *intend* your life more consciously, in order to achieve the desires you want and deserve. Or, you can *react* your way through life, receiving in return whatever your personal vibration determines to be so—be it "good," "bad," or indifferent.

That's right—your situation today is the result of the reality you have created (via your past patterns of thought and consequential emotions), and all of that has patterned together, leading you to this moment. So right now, why not *choose* your new reality by understanding and believing that:

- you *choose* to make changes to your life
- you *choose* how you feel about everything
- you *choose* if you will keep to a chosen Path
- you *choose* to be free of your perceived hardships
- you *choose* to accept that outside people and/or situations do not dictate how you will ultimately feel about yourself and your life
- you *choose* whether you will be joyful or upset, regardless of external situations

...it's all up to *you*. If you believe you are "trapped" in your life situation, or have to wait years for conditions to change (e.g., kids out of school, the need for a certain amount of money in the bank, in a difficult relationship you can't immediately exit, don't have the right job, etc.), then you are traveling a wicked road.

You are flat wrong if you feel you have been victimized, and therefore can only attain a certain level of growth. Maybe no one has ever been this direct with you—but if you don't hear it straight up, you run the risk of living with limiting thoughts and life conditions... *forever!* Do you want that? And do you believe because you were raised in a difficult environment that you can't excel? Well, I'm sure it was very tough, but you need to get over it, because people in your shoes have moved mountains once they "chose to choose themselves" (thank you, James Altucher!). In other words, drop the victim labels and self-defeating attitude, because this level of thinking will only bring you more of the same.

I know moving beyond a painful emotion can and will be very difficult for some of you but, again, how long are you willing to choose that limiting life? And if not now, then when will you release all of that pain? Consider the damage the stress of your victim labels is causing you. Yes, something happened to you in the past (join the club!), but it's the labels you have chosen surrounding that event, which serve to keep you from truly exceling toward your life's purpose. How long will you let these labels define you?

The simple prior examples are common to all of us, and they are also excuses driven by "selur" to keep you in a negative cycle of limitation. True, people don't normally morph overnight into what they want to become by the next morning. So give yourself a break and understand this is a process.

Once you have decided that making changes is essential, you must convert to a constant positive attitude heading into the series of changes you are about to make. You have to prepare yourself to be mentally and emotionally flexible so your previous, outdated thought patterns don't inhibit your momentum.

For example, your goal is to Keep to Your Spiritual Path, right? And knowing you will have to make some shifts in your life, you will be better set up for success if you are open to new ideas prior to simply *trying* to make those shifts. When we try and fail, we become frustrated. So why not circumvent the frustration by preparing yourself ahead of time, knowing you may not "get it" right away. Realize you may not see immediate results.

This process is all about having an open mindset; lighten your psyche by using a fun approach. This way, you feel that sticking to your Path is not such a monumental task. What I mean is, if you believe your spiritual transition will be a "chore," or you call it "work," or you continually use the term "trying" when referring to your journey, you are setting yourself up for future excuses and failure. Then when you encounter a difficult moment, you may drop the notion of spiritual growth, only to fall back to what's comfortable and, unfortunately, painful, because that's what "selur" is totally into. So don't go there! You attract that which you are...

I, personally, have found more success during a transition period when I've refined my approach ahead of time. For instance, I will take a spell and decipher the pros and cons of the change I'm about to cause. And when I decide to pull the trigger on entering a new phase of my life, I clear my primary mental stumbling blocks as much as possible, so I have a better chance of dealing with any obstacles along the way. So really what I'm doing is finding ways to minimize any tumult that might be associated with a big shift I want to make.

As you take those all-important first steps along your own Path, be sure not to bring your prior or current judgmental thinking with you. If you have a tendency to question anything that does not sit well with you, my guess is you are probably doubting some of the concepts in this book, or anything else which may be virgin to you. We discussed in "Belief Three" the importance of reducing limiting thoughts…so keep this in mind as we move forward. Later, we will go deeply into "flexibility," and why this characteristic is the cornerstone of enlightenment. For now, though, do not allow your reflexive instincts to judge new ideas as they come to you. At this point on your journey, it is better to soften your stance, because loads of wonderful new information are heading your way!

No, you probably won't enter your next phase void of all things negative—but having prepared your mind with elasticity for what's to come, you will be in a better position to pop through a challenging moment and emerge on the other side in good shape.

Traversing your new spiritual Path with an open mind is much like raising a child. The best that parents can do is to prepare their kids so they may excel. Parents provide lessons for their children so they can garner the tools to make it to the next step, as unscathed as possible. And I'm doing the same with you here…preparing you beforehand so you will be in the best possible position to excel.

Each morning when you awake, your first thought should be: *I wonder what great things I will experience today?* Regardless of how good or bad your day before may have been, use that day's experiences to achieve growth and excellence for yourself *today*. This kind of mindset should never change; you should be excited each morning for another opportunity to surge forward based on yesterday's lessons. And it is this consistent approach that will help you break through barriers so you can rise to new heights. The competitive edge you hold each day will assist you in solving perceived issues quickly and effortlessly. More importantly, your persistent focus will point you toward the good things in life. So remain steadfast in your positive emotional attitude, because this is what will help you Keep to Your Spiritual Path!

With a fun and easy perspective toward change, you will feel the challenge of a transition to be less daunting. Keeping things light and fun has a way of reducing the perceived anxiety you may feel when faced with change. Remember, it's totally fine to take two steps forward, then one step back…this happens to all of us. The trick is to catch yourself sooner and sooner with the conditioned need to take that backward step. You will eventually reach the point where consistently moving forward becomes a more natural way of life.

Continue to keep your attitude in a good place, and this will better allow positive future results to flow to and through you with greater speed and intensity. And when you begin catching yourself with those tendencies to return to old patterns, use the self-recognition of all the growth you've already achieved as a chance to exalt! It's time to shout out a heartfelt, "THANK YOU!" as your awareness recognizes what you are accomplishing, and how far you've come.

There is great joy in setting spiritual building blocks. You owe it to yourself to allow them to fall into place and, more importantly, to stand upon them!

You determine your success and your growth by defining your attitude both before entering a new phase, and certainly while you are in it. When you embrace living from your soul's perspective by connecting with people, animals, and the environment—instead of always focusing on material things, titles, and labels—you will be in a position to recognize your dharma…your life's purpose.

So, what to do?

I'm glad you asked!

Here it is in black and white:

In the beginning, you only need to honestly commit to a transition process, and to be open and aware of the little miracles happening around you every day. While this newfound awareness continually washes away the stains of negativity from your life, the veil is lifted and clarity sets in. This refreshing and inspiring clarity is represented in your increased joy and appreciation for life, including all of the goodness it offers. And it is this rediscovered joy (which has always been within you), which acts as the forward force with which you will travel. So the energy that initially went into "commitment to the process" has now been converted into effortless, contagious enthusiasm for joy—which, when properly leveraged, compounds exponentially. The joy will take over. Your soul then emerges.

I know those last couple of sentences are big ones, but read them again until you understand them. For these sentences represent the genesis of what you are about to do.

And now, here's a story for you...

I went to high school in Orangevale, California, just outside of Sacramento. During this time, I was fortunate enough to spend my winters skiing with friends in Lake Tahoe. When I was 18, a buddy of mine and I were on the mountain-drive up through the Sierra Nevadas when the snow began suddenly pouring down in huge volumes. We finally had to pull over along the shoulder of the road (along with many other vehicles), so we could chain up my VW Dasher (I loved that car!). Anyway, I opened the hatchback and pulled out my cardboard box of chains, setting them down next to my driver's-side front tire. Using my hands, I swept away some of the deep snow, clearing a space around the tire. I struggled with the chains for a while, trying to make them fit, while cold snow soaked the back of my neck.

But for some reason, I just couldn't make it work. It's very frustrating installing uncooperative chains when you are dealing with the cold, the snow, the digging, the grease, the freezing metal, and, ultimately, the thought of lost ski time. And all of this resulted in a cranky, irritated, bloody-knuckled Spencer. What to do?

Ah, but my internal pleas for help were soon answered by the

Universe in the form of a man showing up who offered my buddy and I some chain-installation services. Of course, I said yes to the man right away. He was wearing a dark-green, hooded snowsuit. All I could see between the massive snowflakes was his huge black beard protruding from the inside of his hood. Never saw the whites of his eyes. He told me he'd install the chains for $35. "Do it," I said. And with that, he went to work on installing my chains, and the warmth of relief began to melt away my grief.

As my buddy and I stood there watching him do his thing, we started feeling much better and aided because this guy was literally rescuing our day. So we stood around and waited and, after about 30 minutes or so, the man came to me and said, "That'll be $50." I was shocked and asked him, "Why? You told us it was only going to cost $35...?"

"Well, the chains were too large for your tires, so I had to cut out some of the links to customize the fit...and this took a lot of extra time and effort."

Ugh! So not willing or wanting to negotiate with the man who had just saved our tails, I reluctantly paid him the $50 from my limited funds. My friend was also short on money (like most 18-year-olds are!), so he couldn't pitch in and help. Once we were off and rolling again, my emotions were mixed. On one hand, we were able to continue up the mountain but, on the other hand, I knew once I purchased my lift ticket, I'd have no funds left for lunch. And that meant I would probably have to go hungry (a horrible thought for a high school kid!). But luckily, my buddy, Mike, sported me an extra sandwich later on in the day.

But here's the thing: In that moment, I wasn't being totally honest with myself. I mean, I thought I was feeling frustrated because I would ski fewer runs, and didn't have enough to eat on this day. But deep down, I felt disappointed in myself because I wasn't prepared for the trip. And my lack of preparation led to lost mountain time and not enough money to buy everything I needed so I could have fun on the trip.

Fortunately, there are two silver linings to this story:

First, that ski-trip experience has become my mantra for being prepared in all aspects of life—whether it be planning for a trip, stocking for a natural disaster, or entering a new phase of my life. Please understand that I do Love and embrace spontaneity—but when it comes to bigger decisions, the more I prepare, the less I have to worry or stress while experiencing the transition. My preparation also allows me to leap forward with a more adventurous spirit. And this mindset naturally manifests a more open viewpoint of the world, which helps to bring forth greater flexibility and opportunity.

Second, I will never forget what happened next on that fateful ski trip: While the gentleman was installing the chains on my tires, I needed to...um...release the water I had been drinking. So I walked over to the guardrail, making sure the coast was clear. About 10 feet in front of me was a grouping of fir trees covered in beautiful, fresh snow. Since the man was taking care of the whole "chain" situation, I was, therefore, in a much better place emotionally...my mind had calmed down. And in that improved state of mind, I was able to take a moment to appreciate the breathtaking scenery that is the Sierra Nevadas. *This is why we come here,* I said to myself, gazing on the fir trees and freshly fallen snow. Then it happened...

As I was finishing my "business," suddenly from behind a tree, a gray wolf jumped out and was standing stoutly right in front of me! Fright instantly jolted into my body. I remained still, though. The gray wolf was so close I could almost reach out and touch him.

The visual of the wolf was breathtaking. The wolf was flanked by the green fir trees, which were cloaked in heavy snow. His platinum coat contrasted brilliantly against the white bank behind him. There was no aggression in his demeanor at all. I was fascinated by his piercing yet gentle light-blue eyes, which will remain forever with me.

His eyes really spoke to me on that fateful day, allowing me to relax. Or maybe we relaxed together...I don't know. We locked eyes for only a few seconds, but for me it seemed like several minutes. We felt a connection to each other because we were in this storm together. Ready to bound onward, he stared at me as if to wish me well, then disappeared as quickly as he arrived.

Needless to say, that wolf left me awestruck. It was the coolest thing that ever happened to me in my young life. Growing up in the woods of Germany, I had already seen Hirsch (elk), Rehbock (roe deer), and wild boar in close proximity. In the U.S., I sometimes saw Roosevelt elk, white-tailed deer, as well as an occasional brown bear. But I had never interacted with wildlife like I had on that day when the wolf appeared. We affected each other. My love for the natural world was already in play on that day, but it now endures deeper because of moments like that.

Because of this single experience, I learned more about preparing for decisions and new phases of life. I also learned when my mind is calm and peaceful, the Universe will shower me with unexpected gifts of all kinds.

STEPPING STONE: As it relates to preparation, let's say you are about six months into your transition phase. And let's say, during these early months of your transition, you are sitting at work. Internally, you are cruising along with your new spiritual practice. You are feeling generally happy because of it, but know you still have much to learn. But the good news is, your newly implemented perspectives are already showing signs of manifestation, and your enthusiasm for life is growing. In fact, in the months since you have been focused on positive energy, you believe that is the reason you signed your new client to a hefty contract. "The Law of Attraction *does* work!" you say. And signing the new client also allowed you to qualify for a larger annual bonus, which you desperately need. And now you are smiling with relief because you are finally starting to see the seeds of your efforts sprout up through your newly fertilized soil.

But then the phone rings…it's your new client calling to tell you he is having second thoughts and wants to cancel out of the newly signed contract. And so what happens? Your anxiety meter instantly starts redlining. Your world is suddenly falling apart. Your bonus is gone! No swimming pool for you, Clark!

So the question is, in this moment, how do you find the daylight, and bring yourself back to a calm space without experiencing a knee-jerk reaction? The answer is simple: use Love. Leverage your newly found *heightened awareness* of how your feelings create your reality. Since Love is the opposite of fear, pivot from that fear to Love and open your emotional wellbeing to the unlimited options of creativity.

Pivoting to Love allows you the creative space to potentially save the new contract you have with your client. So instead of totally freaking out, you thank him for his call, and for voicing his hesitation. Then, making sure you're in a state of relaxed detachment, you calmly ask him a couple of questions, to ensure you fully understand his concerns. Finally, you remind him of why doing business together can help him and his company.

When something of this nature happens, take a pause, stay calm, and sometimes it even helps to chuckle a bit. And this will assist you in derailing any sudden negative thoughts immediately, in order to maintain a state of Love, joy, poise, and calm. Learning to respond to life's little surprises in this manner does take some time and practice. But as I mentioned earlier, as you wash away the stains of negativity, your resulting joy will attract more of the good stuff and, in this case, a preserved client and contract!

Remember, choose Love in every tough moment. No matter how dark things may seem, know Love is always there for you. In a difficult moment, just whisper to yourself: *Love.*

Now you are ready to enter your Path with the understanding of some of the challenges you may face, and how to overcome them when "selur" lashes out. But have no worries because you are a new person. Your wellbeing is front and center. It's time to enter your new Path...

love

BELIEF FIVE
Your Path of Spiritual Exploration
The art of curiosity.

"So, on the spiritual Path a person learns to find this kind
of happiness without needing nice things to happen on
the outside. Rather, you find happiness by being who you
really are. The trick is to regain such a state when you are
grown and have seen the light and dark sides of life."
– Deepak Chopra

What is your destiny *today?*

We have all heard variations of the renowned metaphysical quotes:
"There is no Path to happiness. Happiness is the Path." And *"It is better
to travel well than to merely arrive."* I believe we all define the spiritual
Path in our own terms. I also feel our ultimate purpose here on Earth
is to live in peace and harmony with all things. In this blissful picture
of coexistence, it does seem that we are all ultimately traveling in
the same direction, regardless of our individual spiritual beliefs and
philosophies...does it not? And in this effort, we all have our own
unique roles within humanity. And this means *you* have a special gift,
which only you can provide to the world in your own exceptional way.
Yes...we all have our own unique destiny to fulfill. As Osho wisely
says, "We can't all be painters, otherwise the world would be ugly."

So now you understand that we each have our own *creative*
purpose. And when I say "creative," I don't mean you have to be an

artist, singer, or sculptor to fulfill your divine role on this planet. What I really mean is, you can be creative in the moment. You can be creative in stillness. You can be creative as a homemaker, a chef, a plumber, or even as a college student. To create is to be alive and evolving, no matter your role. Some of us know what our individual purpose is, while others are still waiting for it to present itself. Some still have yet to ask themselves the question, "What is my specific purpose on this planet, and how do I go about fulfilling it?"

I define "the spiritual Path" as learning how to live quietly *in the moment* so, when the time is right, your dharma will present itself to you. And while functioning within your dharma, you are giving back to the Universe, and to all living things, in the specific way that only you can. You then understand the feeling—the *yearning*—to ignite that passion in other people, so they will be open to their own awakenings when their season is right. *Pssst!* Pass it on...

> "A candle loses nothing by lighting another candle."
> - James Keller

While on your Path, what kind of life do you want to lead? When you say you want "Quality of Life," what does that really mean to you? Well, to me, the major component of Quality of Life rests in the present moment. What happens when you are truly present in the moment? There is no time...you simply "are." And in these precious moments of your life, the honey tastes sweeter, and the warm rays of the sun bathe you a little more deeply. Within the power of present-moment awareness, your connection to all things ripens, and your appreciation of the simple things emanates. You notice the miracle of every bird's song, the scent of the ocean, and the fact that your heart beats according to an unseen energy or spirit. Your Quality of Life increases, your joy heightens, and your life begins to unfold as you consciously intend it to.

Noted conservationist John Muir said, "When we try to pick out anything by itself, we find it hitched to everything else in the Universe."

This means each spiritual concept is interconnected and woven together, with each aspect having an impact on the rest. When you live your life with this understanding, you will find it much easier to develop and grow internally and spiritually. So instead of focusing on the concept of "detachment" alone, understand that "detachment" is also connected to "knowing" and "infinite patience." So, realize and experience *detachment* by *knowing* it will come through *infinite patience.* And I know that reducing "limiting thoughts" can be a challenge, but as you practice "non-judgment" and "awareness," you will slowly begin to declutter your mind. And when "limiting thoughts" are few, there is more room to practice "giving and receiving." That then begets Love. We can go on forever with this, but I think you get my drift.

When first beginning your spiritual journey, you will excel at some concepts, but struggle with others. It may seem a bit chaotic as you digest it all. But when your underlying emotion is Love, everything will fall into place for you.

Learn how to honor your life energy by allowing the joy in your soul to be present with each breath you take. If you believe life is "hard," then it will be such! Remember, it is your decision if you want to think this way. But when you look deep within, beyond your internal storms, what you will find is a source of undeniable Love and purity. Drawing from this infinite well, you will become aware of the partnership you can have and enjoy with God.

Honor this relationship by matching your infinite energy (and patience!) with God's infinite abundance. You have the power to create any life you wish—so remain in the present moment, blissfully aware that yesterday is gone, and tomorrow is not yet here. You can't breathe in the past or the future; only in the present moment can we draw in those all-important breaths of life.

Of course, initially, living in the moment is easier understood intellectually than it is emotionally. People talk all the time about "being in the moment," but who really lives this way? Yes, you can intellectually "understand what it means," but unless you make a commitment to "participate" in conscious awareness at all times, you will eventually deviate from your Path. Remember, the quality of your moment is always equal to the quality of your awareness. Being in the moment is to be an observant...to just "be." This means to just simply observe without thought, and to be at peace regardless of what's going on around you. Quiet your mind, elevate your consciousness through awareness, stand up for your wellbeing, and use the moment as an opportunity to learn. Be in the moment and experience a life of *no fears*. You will know you are living in the moment when stress and judgment no longer dictate your life.

The Path is an ever-evolving meandering way filled with spirited practice, awakenings, joy, epiphanies, peace, and enlightenment. As your mind becomes more flexible and open, your Path will eventually take you to places that, today, you cannot yet comprehend. The indescribable joy of an awakening is a precious gift. If you have had an "awakening," you understand what I mean. If not, remain open and patient and one will come to you. You cannot force the awakenings or "quantum moments" to happen. Just simply Keep to Your Spiritual Path, and your "epiphanies" will arrive on time, when they are supposed to. They will come when you least expect them to, and when you are in a vulnerable state to properly receive them. It is a beautiful experience...

As you read, apply, and practice various spiritual philosophies, you will come across many concepts which impact you immediately. Other ideas or mantras might feel right, but you may not quite understand how to apply them, or how to fit them into your current level of thinking. But if you pick just one concept (for me, detachment comes to mind), you can then ask questions, think about it, talk about it, and listen to any content having to do with it. Then one day when you least expect it, a jolt of energy will blast through you! Something will just click in your mind, and the concept you previously struggled with will instantly become a part of your fabric—you'll just "get it"! And the beauty and abundance felt in that moment, regarding that particular concept, will now be forever with you.

You can then use the juice from that awakening as an accelerant on your Path! And as you continue to walk your Path, other concepts will continue to fall into place for you. And as this happens, the quality of your awareness will elevate, and your need to judge outside conditions will begin to decrease, resulting in an *increased* ability to better handle all of life's many situations. And through this manner of living, you will innately feel a higher degree of contentment.

Here is my formula for spiritual exploration:

In order for you to have growth while continuing along your Path, you are going to have to do things a little differently. As I've already discussed, you will more likely struggle if you have a negative attitude, or if you are unwilling to lighten up. In that vein, look at the spiritual shift you are trying to make as an "exploration." I Love this perspective! Think back to the days of Leif Ericson (Newfoundland), Christopher Columbus (the Caribbean), "Buzz" Aldrin (the moon), and, my favorite, Sir Ernest Shackleton (Antarctica). These pioneering explorers were all driven in part by one profound concept: *curiosity.*

In other words, they all shared the desire to "learn." They observed life with an inner thirst for knowledge. They took notes as they went, and tracked their progress. They were open-minded and lived in the moment, unafraid of mystery. So why not develop your own sense of curiosity? Ask more questions. Scratch your head a bit and get creative in your endeavors. Become an explorer and embark on the mysterious quest, which will eventually provide the answers you seek.

And I'm sure you're wondering, "But where can curiosity lead me...?"

To ultimate enlightenment or, as otherwise stated, complete "God-consciousness."

Yes, the answers to your questions and the reconditioning of your thought patterns will sooner or later lead you to that "place." You will eventually learn that walking your Path in stillness will lead you "there." You become still by decluttering your mind. You declutter your mind by practicing active awareness. You practice active awareness by no longer "spectating" your way through life. Instead, you consciously "participate."

Now try thinking about this philosophy in reverse: For example, when you feel pressure at work, be conscious in that moment by allowing yourself to feel the initial signs of the stress. Now participate in your life by elevating your awareness of how you are beginning to feel. Through this heightened awareness, keep your composure. Remain still. Remain calm. Smile. Don't allow your cyclical thoughts to run wild, because this will only increase your level of stress. Instead, just stay in the moment where there is no time and no fear. Look for the daylight, shine it, and stay creative. Now with your decluttered mindset in place, simply and poetically handle the situation with poise and grace.

Conscious participation

↓

Active awareness

↓

Decluttering your mind

↓

Stillness

↓

God-consciousness

You see, conscious participation allows you to consider whether you are "habitually reacting" or "calmly responding" to life's situations. And whether you choose to react or respond, this dictates your thoughts, which in turn produces your feelings. And since this is a *feeling* Universe, you will, through Law of Attraction, receive what you are ultimately feeling. So why not consciously participate in your moments by elevating the quality of your awareness?

Your acute awareness allows you to remain flexible in the moment, keeping your mind peaceful and decluttered. And when your decluttered mind remains still and/or imaginative, this increases the chances of you having a higher-quality moment. Learn to live this way and you will eventually reach ultimate enlightenment, and/or you will become God-realized.

What is God-realized, you ask? I believe it to be living in a perpetual state of true Love, devoid of any negative thoughts or destructive emotions. Some of you have experienced these moments, but to live this way on a more consistent basis is our goal.

Within our spiritual practice, we have to be careful how we define certain terms. Being on a Path indicates we are on our way to some place better than where we are now. But what's more important than "now"? Begin to digest the concept that you are already "here." So be at peace with where you are "now," because it is in this moment that you are simultaneously feeling the beauty of your growth, while elevating your level of consciousness.

It is also important to understand that our Western culture may have you believing there is always something greater to attain in the form of accumulation—whether it be material things, or labels we place upon one another. Indeed, our Western society seems to dictate that once we have what we desire, we must then continue to ask ourselves, "What's next?" And in this ego-driven need for "more," we're never satisfied.

"Some people are so poor all they have is money."
– Maureen Gill

Yes, you are on a journey. And along this journey, you are unlearning the old, conditioned, outdated way in which you used to think while, in chorus, allowing your soul's full potential to come forth. The irony of it all is that your soul already knows everything "you" are trying to "learn." So now we are getting into the whole "who you are" aspect. Are you two entities—your soul and your Self? Or are you comprised of your soul and the labels you have *about* yourself? Well, one thing is for certain: You are your soul—that's it! However, you have certain coatings draped around you, which need to be shed so you can live more fully from your soul's perspective. And walking your Path serves as the evaporation of your coatings, allowing your soul to come forth.

Your path to visualization…

Have you given any thought to how your Path may appear? I'm a visual learner so I don't just *feel* my Path, I see it as well. My Path begins with a beautiful arbor, covered with purple wisteria vines. The arbor's gate is of rustic iron. There are Montana-slate stepping stones, which lead me through the gate. Then there is blue-star creeper growing low, surrounding pink heather plants. American robins are perched and singing. There is a maple tree-shaded fountain splashing to the right, with majestic mountains anchored to the left. The sky is blue with a few billowing clouds. Canadian geese are flying overhead. My vision is peaceful and fertile. For me, my Path is sanctuary.

This is the image of my simple Path. It's the place I am every day. I wonder what's around the next corner, knowing my practice will guide me through. This philosophy works for me. Try spending some time creating a visualization of your own Path, so you will want to walk it with each breath you take. Visualizing your Path is an important step on your journey; otherwise your path is just a notion or an undefined entity, which may keep you aimless.

To construct a visualization of how your own Path might look, try this exercise: First, close your eyes, and visit an outdoor space in your mind that you really Love. Lose yourself in the feeling of why this natural area is so special to you. Now imagine you are standing at your Path's front gate. Develop this image in your mind's eye, maybe by borrowing from other beautiful places you have been, or wish to visit. Is your front gate a trailhead to a mountain path you frequently hike? Or maybe it is the mouth of a serene desert highway? At any rate, spend whatever time you need nurturing the visual image of your Path's gateway. This vision will develop over time as you practice your visualization each day.

Now that you have an image of your Path, it's important to be in the right frame of mind as you enter and begin to walk upon it. Understand we, as humans, are continually in the process of rebirthing ourselves. So you can either start at your gate's entrance every day, or simply begin where you left off on your Path the day before. As you walk your first steps, take a deep breath and give immense gratitude for everything you have in your life. Then make sure you bring yesterday's learned lessons with you while you move forward in the moment.

Since you are your soul, keep your eyes directed toward the source from whence you came. Remember, you are a part of God, and God is always within you, so use this idea as the foundation of your daily visualizations. You will always know what to do as long as you let your intuition guide you. Buy into spirituality 100 percent. Anything less and your present circumstances will remain the same (or they will only change at a much slower rate). Facing the gate (or your next step on the Path) is to "be." It's not a matter of reconnecting to God; the connection is and always has been there.

Your new spiritual practice will eliminate the stagnation you may be feeling in your life, reopening the flow of abundance *through* you, not *to* you. You see, true abundance lies in giving and receiving (we will go over this in greater detail later). With each step you take on your Path, walk with purpose, enhancing your connection with God and all living things, by living with participatory awareness.

Continue to look for opportunities to apply what you are learning. Remember, have fun searching for moments to exercise a new lesson or teaching. Revel in the feeling of "it works!" Recognize the Universe in action. Make notes of your progress so, during those challenging times, you can look back and remember all the moments when you witnessed the direct results of your new discipline. This will help you Keep to Your Spiritual Path, allowing you to build momentum while doing so. And you build momentum and stick to your Path by allowing yourself to be vulnerable, meaning you stay open to new ideas coming to you and from you.

Walking a path of infinite patience...

Learn to get out of your own way. Know you are abundant, completely and always! Your Path is ample and always giving...you just have to open your mind to receive its gifts. Don't worry about the "when and how." Just live moment to moment, and continue to practice detachment to the results you desire, thereby reducing and vaporizing your stress levels. Bear in mind that the "when and how" will take care of itself through the process of infinite patience. So instead of fretting with, "How much longer is this going to take?" try shifting to, "Because I've requested and am co-creating my life with God, I'm one day closer to the desires I want and deserve!" This simple shift in thinking will change the way you feel, allowing for more detachment to take place.

And that brings up an interesting reflection. You may being saying, "But I'm usually terribly impatient, and now you want me to suddenly have *infinite* patience? *No way!*" Remember, a belief is nothing more than a thought repeated over and over again. So if you keep telling yourself you have no patience, well…you will continue to have no patience. Try telling yourself the exact polar opposite of that limiting belief, then begin to believe in the new *unlimited* belief, and watch your life change for the better! Increased patience equals decreased stress. Eliminate those dreadful limiting thoughts by realizing your enormous potential!

Remember, this is a process by which you will learn to stop installing those self-defeating roadblocks. As you take each step along your Path, in your own time, you will feel less of a need to judge, and this will lead to a less-cluttered life. Combine that with repeating your resonating mantras throughout your day. This opens your eyes to seeing the little miracles all around you. More importantly, you will be bringing goodness and Love into your existence like never before. Soon you will wonder how you did not recognize the power of your feelings, and their ability to attract and create your life experiences. Once you remove those habitual, limiting blinders, it all becomes so obvious!

So with infinite patience you will come to realize a life with less stress, and your attachment to the anxiety of what you *don't* have will, therefore, be significantly reduced. So what does that do for you? It decreases your daily emotional turbulence! And suddenly, your dreams do not seem so far away. But the cool part is, the concept of infinite patience starts to become plausible for you. Then one day (again, when you least expect it), you'll have another epiphany and say to yourself, "Wow! Things are really coming to me! I *can* have infinite patience! I *do* have the ability to intend and create the life I desire!"

And it's exactly this kind of realization, which allows you to walk your Path with excitement, curiosity, and exploration every day. It's a wonderful phenomenon!

STEPPING STONE: Here is a fun exercise I do every day: First, create in your mind your perfect life image (how your life might look if all areas of it were ideally as you'd like them to be). Then, spend 18 minutes of quiet time really getting into the details. Now write down 10 key elements of your dream life (or 10 "keynotes," if you will). Keep these details to yourself, not sharing them with anyone (this will give you complete freedom to illustrate your dream life without having to be concerned about what anybody else might think). Now, relax your mind into a place where you can actually smell the freshly mowed lawn surrounding your dream home. See the ancient mortar between the stones that cement the castle walls. Lookout onto the hazy sunset of the countryside where your new home resides. You may even want to experience in your mind, for example, working in the café of a small European town, serving treats and smiles. Or perhaps you'll want to visualize yourself on a fabulous stage, speaking your messages of truth to the masses. Whatever you dreams may be, just go to a quiet place, and sink into the feeling tone of actually "living" those dreams. And make it a priority to practice these kinds of visualizations every day, and soon enough you will begin to feel what it's like to actually turn those dreams into reality!

Now, with pen and paper (forget about the computer), write down the steps you actually need to take in order to get closer to your dreams. Forget for a moment your current circumstances, and just write down your plan as if you are going to pull the trigger one year from today. Don't worry about what you are leaving behind in your current life. Just consider the steps you need to take in order to move forward. The best part about practicing this exercise is that the simple act of planning your dream life will put you in a great frame of mind!

Live your life in your mind as if you are executing the steps you need to take to make your next move. Allow yourself to visualize in great detail of what it feels like to be executing your plan. Is it exciting? Refreshing? Magnificent? Make sure you allow your feelings of joy to spring to the surface as you are living your dream life right inside your own thoughts, while detailing it all on paper. We escape our realities all the time by watching movies or TV—or by fumbling through our to-do lists, all in an attempt to distract ourselves from our unmet desires. So why not use your own desires and dreams to escape instead? The big difference with *this* exercise is it will actually lead you to attainment (as opposed to giving you yet another excuse as to why you're still not "living the good life").

To really begin manifesting your desires, here's something else you can do: Recall those 10 keynotes I asked you to write down. Well, start carrying that list with you everywhere you go. And every morning (twice a day is even better!), stop for 10 minutes and read through your list. Take some deep breaths while you do it…slow down…close your eyes…block out the whole world and just focus on the first item. Spend a full minute or so using all of your senses to experience it. Then, do the same for the rest of the items on your list. Really *feel* your visualization…the more you tell yourself your new story, the more you will begin to fill in the little blanks of how to make it all happen! And then, suddenly, before you know it, you will be rounding out your dream! That's right—you'll actually be meeting your new neighbors while moving into that country dream house of yours; you'll be serving the regulars at the local cafe in the small European town; you may even be giving your first talk to a hundred people or more at your local bookstore. And wouldn't *that* be incredible!

So keep in mind, you are telling a "new" story here; thinking and looking forward to the future, while simultaneously grounding yourself in the awareness of the present moment. So tell yourself these fresh and positive stories, feel fantastic while you do it, and let goodness and abundance flow through you. The beauty of this exercise is it helps you to feel great!

Two monumental things are happening for you during the course of this exercise: First, you are creating joy for yourself, and you are also beginning the manifestation process of your dream life. And as you grow spiritually, you will realize your well-defined dreams are attainable and, in fact, expected. Through infinite patience, you will realize all of your dreams...they will come to you when the season is right.

Who cares what they think?

Keep to Your Path by living with the mindset of breathing each moment from your soul's perspective. Forget about what other people think of you or your dreams. When you get all wrapped up in what other people might be thinking about your process, that's "selur" talking. So forget about acting in a certain way, or saying things just to fit in. Stop worrying about what people might say about you. Other people's opinions (especially the naysayers who aren't yet on the spiritual Path) are trivial, and have no bearing on your wellbeing. I mean, who cares what they think? What does their opinion have to do with your journey? You certainly do not need their approval to validate your life and the Path you have selected.

Other people may not understand you, but this is only because they have not yet asked themselves the questions you are now asking. You are simply further along in your conscious development than they are—know that these people will find their own journey, in their own way, and in their own timeframe...just as you did.

I remember feeling reluctant to tell people when I first began meditating, because of the potential judgment I thought I would feel from them. Then one day I just spit it out! And the reaction I received was actually quite positive. I realized speaking of spirituality is not such a huge stigma anymore. More and more people are opening their minds to it. So as time went on, I became less apprehensive of people's reactions toward my own spiritual journey. Today, I'm delighted to mention to others that I walk a spiritual Path, and that I meditate every day, because this may lead to a nice conversation in which we all learn something. Or maybe the conversation might even lead to a new inspiration, a new lesson, or even to a new friend.

Recently, I had a discussion with two delightful people at a coffee shop. Rick is a psychologist, and his wife, Linda, a former attorney. Linda now assists Rick in his psychological practice. Because this was the first time we ever met, they had no way of knowing about my spirituality. In asking Rick about his practice, he told me how diet can change the way people respond to medication and treatment, making the formerly "incurable" patients now potentially "curable." We then shifted the topic, speaking of those people who don't know where to begin when there is a desire to turn their lives around. I then made the comment that when people simply begin with gratitude and giving, they open themselves up to the abundance life has to offer. Then I posed a few other ideas, which helped to tie together my whole philosophy.

After a brief pause, Rick looked at me and said, "You are certainly an evolved soul." I happily and modestly embraced his compliment, moving onto the next subject.

My motivation for telling you about my conversation with Rick and Linda is to show you the positive results that come from walking a conscious Path. Back in the "old days," my advice to people looking for help probably would have been, "Just get a grip and move on." But today, I'm able to step back and be truly compassionate; I'm inspired for all the right reasons.

Being driven by the wrong motives (control, labels, fear, greed—the type of car you drive, the neighborhood in which you live, how you or other people dress) will more than likely have a negative impact on your spiritual growth. Conversely, your ability to be unaffected by other people's opinions is a humongous step in the right direction. The freedom you feel when you release those unhealthy motivations is very liberating. When you attain the car, the house, and the clothing you desire from a spiritually healthy perspective, that's when you can truly say you are "living your dream." Remember, life's conditions and other people's opinions don't determine your wellbeing…you do! Your perceptions are your choice.

Walking your Path is the process you must undergo to retrain your mind and wash away the stains of old, conditioned thought patterns. Once you get to a certain point on your Path, and you start seeing the fruits of your newfound awareness, you will not allow yourself to ever go back to your old ways of living. Walking the spiritual Path is a beautiful, new way of life. You define your destiny by your spiritual growth with each step you take. So give and feel gratitude for your evolution, and use the momentum you build to shed each subsequent layer. Feel yourself becoming lighter every day. Feel the abundant connection to all living things. Feel the warmth which is God. Walk your Path cleanly.

> "To move, to breathe, to fly, to float,
> to gain all while you give.
> To roam the roads of lands remote,
> to travel is to live!"
> – Hans Christian Andersen

Walking your Path can, at times, be tumultuous...and that is a beautiful thing. Remember, we learn when we are challenged. There are times, however, when we need a little help. In this chaotic, frazzled, and speedy world, it's important to find some quiet time, is it not? How often do you find yourself wishing for a little peace, or maybe even trying to carve out a few minutes for yourself here and there? I know I certainly crave this kind of alone time...for me there is no greater place to experience tranquility than in Nature.

BELIEF SIX
Nature's Inspiration

The sanctuary of the womb.

Ah…the awesome haven of Nature. No matter the challenges you are facing, there is no better cure than to give yourself to the waiting arms of the natural world. To walk a forest's trail is to connect to sacredness. Allow its pure canopy to envelop you. Put your hands on a massive cedar tree and connect with its coursing energy and magnificent splendor. Then pause for a moment, offering profound thanks for what that single tree gives to you. It's in moments like this when we realize *we* belong to Mother Earth, not the other way around. And this puts our existence here on Earth in proper perspective.

Sit on a log and take from your pack nothing but your ability to observe. Soak in the sounds… First, you may hear nothing. Then you pick up the subtle yet apparent breeze gently whispering through the branches. Next, the songs of chickadees and the shriek of a woodpecker suddenly surround you. Then, maybe you're able to tune into the cleansing roar of a nearby river. Strangely, in an unassuming way, you start to realize the weight of the world has dissipated since your appreciation of Nature's purity has taken over.

The more time you spend in Nature, the more your innate understanding of how life teems in the forest surfaces in your consciousness. Your senses are heightened. You smile. You feel safe as you contemplate the ancient principles of balance associated with the natural world. No one can teach you this...you just instinctively know it. Eventually you grow to admire it. You can just feel it. You are bonded with it. Its impact nourishes your very Being. Allow the real balance of Nature to flood your senses, opening your mind to how you can live your life in a similar way. Mother Earth gives Herself freely and unconditionally to you. And in return you take from Her great inspiration, while giving back immense respect and Love. You know now what to do.

Have you ever wondered about the origin of Nature's calming effect? Consider what you see when you look at a tree...you notice the bark, the branches, the pine needles, and pinecones. You may see sunlight streaming through or, if you are exceptionally fortunate, an owl peering from a burrow in the trunk. But realize this: It is in that "labeling" of the tree, and the things you see *associated* with the tree, which stifles your innate ability to experience Nature's calming effect. Conversely, when you observe the natural world in its totality, through a statement of *presence*, you are able to feel the awesomeness which is and can only be Mother Nature.

Nature gives all of its splendor without asking for reciprocity; the energy of Nature helps you to establish your initial bearings as you face life's many challenges. Are you having a tough time getting motivated to change? Or are you finding it difficult to get started? Well, you don't need to look any further than to Nature for inspiration. For a variety of reasons, we sometimes "get in our own way," making life more difficult for ourselves than it has to be. In those moments, a trip to your favorite park, or a walk along a frequented trail, can help you to become more present in your life. Soon you'll see...Nature has a way of rinsing away the damaging blight of negative thought patterns.

When you become present in Nature, your awareness can create the space for you to be inspired by its natural balance and calming effect. If you are a little more stubborn and don't have the drive to become that present, Nature will still have its effect on you...all on its own. When you are in the presence of the ocean, for example, breathe it in and try becoming a part of it. Notice the water lapping effortlessly onto the shore, every time, without fail. The steadiness of the surf provides the peace for which you search. The salt air represents a fresh start, giving you freedom and a clean slate. The awesomeness of the ocean's power will give you a sense of wonder and, before you know it, your outlook will begin to shift.

Use that creative space to look up and notice the clouds blowing across the sky, or to watch a raccoon drunkenly delight in a plum from your backyard tree. In this simple state of observation, notice how you feel the lessening of fear-based thought patterns and emotions. Why? Because when you are present with the Mother, there is no time…and you are only left to observe, appreciate, and bask in Her beauty. You will feel the profound effect this has on you as the quality of your awareness begins to increase. And it's in stringing together these moments of beauty that you establish a new way of life, which then serves to suffocate those negative thought patterns.

Learn to stay in this awe-inspiring, present headspace of Nature for just a few minutes, and feel your perspective begin to organically shift in a positive direction. Just allow those natural moments to be. Let Nature consume you. Ask yourself: *How many times have I been awestruck by the natural world?* Now allow yourself to seek daily opportunities to evolve spiritually when you simply witness an earthworm crawling on wet pavement; or beams of sunlight casting themselves through the trees; or your beautiful, soulful pet asking for some loving attention.

Make observing Nature a part of your daily experience. When you do this, you will no longer complain about the weather. Instead you will come to appreciate yet another cold, rainy day, or the eighteenth day in a row of scorching 101-degree heat. You'll even learn to relish one more afternoon of shoveling a foot of snow from your driveway! You will see the miracles of such days, as Nature's cumulative effect on you creates a peacefulness within your Being. And with this feeling at your core, you will have a more stable foundation from which to draw during those difficult moments. The peace of Nature can become part of your natural fabric. And the peace of Nature's qualities then emanate from within you, which can serve as a major source of inspiration for you. Keep Nature's energy close to you, and draw on it whenever you need it. In fact, draw on it all day long so you are ahead of the game, keeping negativity at bay.

Here is a real-life story about how Nature helped me:

I have always appreciated the fresh air and the magnificence of all things natural. I was introduced to the forests of central Germany by my grandpa at a very early age. He taught me about wildlife's habitat, diet, and movements. He spoke of forest management and overall respect for Nature. So, many years ago, I began walking and hiking in Nature as a form of exercise, and as a way to commune with Earth's creatures.

In 2005, here in the U.S., I was growing a small business and dealing with the same life complexities we all share. Typically, during this time, I started out my morning walks by thinking about each issue I had on my plate—not so much trying to solve them, but simply talking them through in my mind. Eventually, though, I just started taking in the surrounding inspiring scenery during my walks.

Well, after a few months of this, I noticed an amazing result from my walks: My pinball-machine-of-a-mind, which I carried onto the trail with me each morning, was somehow reshuffled and reorganized into clear and more concise categories. It was like my mind had calmed down enough to where it was much easier for me to find solutions to the many issues that plagued me. Yes, Nature had, all on its own, decluttered my chaotic mind! This was a huge revelation for me, and a big lesson along my own spiritual journey. My walks in Nature were actually teaching me how to "be"…how to just simply *be.* I learned at that pivotal time in my life that I didn't really need to *search* for solutions; the answers I sought just came to me when the time was right. So, in the long run, opening my heart to the serenity of Nature allowed me to see life in much clearer terms.

I think it's important to look at Nature as the prime indicator of a balanced Universe. So instead of just seeing the trees, consider the life of an entire, unified forest: The sun warms a pinecone, asking for nothing in return. Feeling that warmth, the pinecone opens and offers its seed to the receiving soil. The soil, already rich

Be You to Full [handwritten marginalia]

with nutrients from past generations, provides a home for the seed in which to nestle. Then the rainclouds bring a drink. A sapling has germinated from the seed and sets its taproot. Slowly, it begins reaching for the daylight (there's that word again!). But it doesn't "struggle" to grow; it just stretches for the sky, bending in the wind, and sharing space with its fellow saplings.

Over time, the saplings become the new forest, while the parent trees return to the ground from whence they came, nourishing the soil for the next seeds of opportunity. This is Nature's inspiration. Nature gets along with itself because it just "is." Ask yourself: *What can I learn from Nature?* Maybe you can learn to get along better with yourself, and with those around you as well.

When you observe Nature for a few present moments, don't think about anything else. Just look at your surroundings with no expectations or judgment on what you see. As you practice this kind of observation each day, the idea of "not thinking" will become intuitive for you...and this will lead you to utter peace. The grass is singing as its roots soak up a summer rainfall. Take a look at an indoor plant sitting on a shelf...just observe it. Be aware of the life that single plant leads. Be in the moment. Allow the peace of the natural world to flow through you. You already have it within you, but it's up to you to let it emerge. Take a deep breath or two... Do you *feel* it?

> "Once you have heard the meadowlark and
> caught the scent of fresh-plowed earth,
> peace cannot escape you."
> – Sequichie

Nature is effortless; it just happens. It allows everything to come and go in its "is-ness" (thank you, Eckhart Tolle!). And in Nature's "is-ness," nothing struggles, so why should you? Lao Tzu teaches us no storm will last forever.

When you emulate Nature, you learn to open your mind. If you remain flexible like a palm tree bending in the wind, you keep your emotional turbulence at bay. Don't remain rigid in your thinking, allowing yourself to snap like a dead, dry branch.

One thing that can really help you on your Path is if you visit Nature each day in person or in your mind. Just allow yourself to sink into it. Peace…

STEPPING STONE: Go now and take a walk in the natural world. Feel your anxiety immediately dissipate when you first enter the forest. Maybe begin a new hobby, which requires you to be in the woods more often. Learn to bushcraft using natural materials instead of plastic, nylon, or metal. Or use your talents in another way by collecting nuts, pinecones, and fallen branches to create arrangements with which to decorate your home and to give as gifts. Or if you are reading at night as I often do, close your eyes and imagine walking your favorite path, or perhaps think of a scene you often enjoy from a window or deck. Remember, Nature can allow your mind to do its thing; to work through the process of re-categorizing itself to feel more peaceful. Look to Nature, live with flexibility and Love, and your joy will be palpable.

Invest in yourself with this simple and beautiful routine of returning to and reconnecting with the natural world. Remember, Nature is always in balance; it gives and receives with infinite patience. So carry its harmony with you all day, and watch your life miraculously change. The "natural" life is the one you are meant to lead. I'm opening your eyes to the opportunity (and its subsequent benefits) for you to do as Nature does.

Clouds just move
Wind just blows
Leaves just flutter
Grass just grows
—STK

Simple, huh? "Yes, I agree. But tell me, Spencer, how am I going to do all of this cool stuff…?"

BELIEF SEVEN
I Believe you have it within you

Establishing the footing of your Path.

The crux of this book's philosophy is to provide you with tools so, in a challenging moment, you will be able to handle any situation with ease…allowing you to continually evolve along your spiritual Path. To open this book and apply its contents is to accept its information, and to honor your desire to reach your highest potential. This book is a tool that, when combined with other teachings and applications, can elevate your life experience. Learn to live in the moment with expertise and you will enjoy a sublime, abundant life.

Journeying along your Path will put you in position to receive life's information, so you may lace it all together, creating a *knowing* that you are blossoming into and toward enlightenment. You must set yourself up to have fewer (or no) limiting beliefs and emotional blocks which get in the way of your ultimate desires. Live this way and you will grow magnificently.

I'm often asked: "How do I get 'from here to there'?" Or: "How do I *not* get angry when *that* happens?" These are very normal and natural questions, because you are looking through the only life lens you have ever known. You have been taught by society to "react" to situations of all types. You, much like the rest of the population, are simply a bundle of conditioned reflexes—and your habitual behavior has been perpetually reinforced by your family, friends, and the society around you. But because we have been taught over the generations to behave in and think a certain way, understand what works well for some, doesn't necessarily work well for others. So why not ask some questions, and/or live your life based on your own unique desires? Why not counteract cultural training by opening your mind and becoming flexible so you can uncoil your conditioned reflexes, and morph them into conscious, participatory involvement? This simply means you are training yourself to live from your purest perspective…from that of your soul.

So what are the steps you have to take on your journey to get "there"? Well, first and foremost, you have to understand "there" doesn't really exist. The height of spiritual evolution and the metaphorical "there" are not exactly the same thing. You are already "here." You only have this moment, and that is it. So what do you intend on doing with it? If you want to create and mold yourself into a masterpiece—into the best "you" possible—continue to look inward for growth. The journey within is a conscious moment-by-moment endeavor. And yes, it will take some time for you to evolve and to reduce your limiting beliefs. But if you are always trying to get "there," you will never "arrive." Because, you see, "there" is actually "here." This being said, why not release the need to "arrive," and turn your attention toward recognizing the precious nature each moment has to offer.

Remember, though, this is a fun and exciting time in your life! You will see and *feel* immediate results as long as you remain open to the process. Every morning when you awake, ask yourself: *What great things will happen today?* Your dream life is waiting for you as you co-create with absolute intent. Remember, this is your beautiful Path.

Laying the groundwork for a fruitful and committed journey along your Path will require much self-reflection. And there are three principles which will tee you up for your new practice:

- Awareness
- Participation
- Aligning with goodness

Awareness is your catalyst!

The fundamental principle to Keeping to Your Spiritual Path is to develop a heightened sense of awareness; this is your greatest asset. Awareness helps tremendously in positioning your emotional shifting; it allows you the space to remain loving without habitually reacting to any given situation. Without awareness, nothing changes. But *with* awareness, you are able to determine the ways in which you can better manage your life, while having the ability to evaluate the state of your emotions within various situations. And when you are aware of your emotions, you can either maintain a certain course of action, or choose to deviate down a different road. So you see, a heightened level of awareness can allow you to better intend your life's outcomes.

Your awareness provides you with the ability to create a healthy space between your wellbeing and a low-energy situation. *Through* awareness, you are now buffered from just routinely reacting, thereby providing yourself with the opportunity to remain calm and positive during a challenging moment. And when you are in a positive, loving place you, in return, offer more imaginative and peaceful responses.

In the end, it is really your awareness that allows you to be appropriately receptive to new concepts—or even with challenging circumstances—because emotional awareness engenders an open mind. And an open mind is your spirit in action. Openness gives rise to flexibility; it allows your soul to begin breaking through those old, tired layers, which have built up over your lifetime. Sure, you will grow at your own rate but, as you participate in the process of heightening your awareness, you will begin to feel a surrounding force-field of positive energy, which can repel the damaging issues from your life experience.

Your awareness acts as your "keel," and can keep you from capsizing in the midst of turbulent circumstances. Consider, for a moment, the functions of a vessel's keel: It's a structural element—a beam—around which the hull of a ship is constructed. The keel runs down the middle of the ship from bow to stern. It serves as a foundation (or "spine," if you will), providing major structural strength and lateral support. It normally marks the beginning of a ship's construction.

And like a ship, your spiritual growth and practice must be built around the quality of your awareness (or your "keel," as it were). So your personal keel will help you to maintain your "true north," because it runs through the middle of your Path, from your first step to your next. It serves as the foundation of your practice. Develop your sense of conscious awareness and revel in the beauty of uncoiling your past training, thereby allowing the subsequent emergence of your soul. Remember, it's your awareness that wakes you up when "selur" is stirring the pot of fear.

Participating versus spectating...

With your new level of awareness intact, you will realize you have been "spectating" your way through life. "Spectating" means you are trying your best to handle life's ups and downs—but because you've had the same cyclical thoughts over a long period of time, this means you are probably reacting your way through life, without a lot of consciousness around what your habitual reactions are creating. And so one day blends into the next, as your dreams go unnoticed, and your desires remain unrealized. And where has this gotten you? Wouldn't you agree there's much more to life than this unconscious way of behaving?

So how do you stop "spectating" and instead begin "participating"? *Egad!* What does that even mean? Well, it's really quite simple: You *stop* spectating and *start* participating through the process of self-awareness, of course! *This is where you close the chasm between "want" and "belief." This is the moment when you begin to intentionally create the circumstances of your own life experience.* With self-awareness comes a life shift, and the potential of positive change. Become self-aware by being more conscious of your interpretation of the information bombarding you *and* your subsequent emotional status as that information comes toward you. In other words, how are you handling those difficult moments? If you are like most people, you are simply reacting without giving the quality of your wellbeing any real attention.

And in that unconscious moment, you're not allowing yourself to calmly sort out the information being presented to you, which means you'll probably react defensively, without much thought as to the outcome you're going to produce as such. Many times, this can make the situation much worse. You have to be careful in these types of circumstances, as you become aware that "selur" is trying to gain momentum by taking your thoughts quickly down a dark and dangerous alley. But when you are actively *participating* in your life's circumstances, you can better stay in the moment, which gives you the conscious space to consider more creative alternatives.

Remind yourself of *Why?* you believe in your spiritual journey. Recall the feeling of what it means to set a building block within your foundation, and create opportunities for yourself to recognize the miracles of each day.

Train yourself to become self-aware so you can handle situations with ease. Self-awareness is the genesis of "participating," and will lead you into a more consciously engaged life. As you become self-aware, you will discover that *everything is as it should be.* Remember, the Universe is always in balance—meaning the result of your current situation is exactly what you have drawn into your life via your thought patterns and their associated emotions. That's right—you have allowed every condition you are experiencing to come to you in divine order. I'm sure many of you are resistant to this notion, and that is actually quite normal. You may be saying, "I'm sorry, Spencer, but there's no way I'm responsible for *that!*"

But here's the thing: If you believe in the Law of Attraction, you cannot be selective in your evaluation of what you have drawn to yourself. Therefore, your life circumstances are the result of what you have directly (or *indirectly*) propagated to the Universe. And this is a very hard truth for many people to digest. But the sooner you align yourself with this Law's impact, the sooner you can move forward in a positive way. Become a friend of intent!

Now let's get back to life's challenging situations:

When you are having a difficult moment, that challenge usually goes down in about a millisecond! But by bringing calm, participatory awareness into that challenging millisecond, this then allows you to enter the problem-solving space with a level head, so you can put together a creative approach, and ultimately be in a more peaceful place. So the challenging moment is actually an opportunity to stand up for your wellbeing. And this is what life is all about! Since maintaining a healthy, balanced wellbeing is your ultimate goal, it's important to bring participatory awareness into your many life's circumstances sooner, rather than later.

I recently listened to a wonderful story from Claudia's 82-year-old mother, Ligia, regarding how she uses a particular mantra to handle life's challenging moments. When she was a young, 18-year-old student attending prep school in Colombia, she sat down at the lunch table on the first day of the new school year. On their plates, all of the girls were given a lunch of rice, salad, chicken, and lentils. Well, Ligia gladly ate all of it—except the lentils. "I hate lentils!" she exclaimed.

When the mid-afternoon snack came, all of the girls were given a banana and a glass of milk. Ligia, though, was asked to go to the main dining hall by herself, where her lunch plate was still sitting on the table, right where she had left it. And her lentils remained! She had refused to eat them earlier, so no snack for Ligia! Even so, Ligia still refused to eat her lentils.

Now it was dinner time. All of the girls were given their fresh dinner—except for you-know-who. So there was Ligia, once again staring down the lentils, which were still on the same plate. What do you think she did? Yup, it was a no-go on the lentils. All of the girls found themselves enjoying their delicious meals, while Ligia sat in front of her now-crusty lentils…with a few tears running down her cheeks. She went to bed hungry that night.

Not knowing what to expect the next morning, she headed into the dining hall, only to see on the table her same plate from the day before—lentils intact! But this time she decided to cooperate by eating the lentils. From that moment on, she ate her meals completely, without complaint.

The impact this lesson had on Ligia throughout her long, healthy life is this: She transformed a difficult experience into a positive mantra for herself, which served her well when she needed it. With each challenge she faced throughout her subsequent six-plus decades, she would say to herself, "Another plate of lentils." That was her way of saying, "Everything is as it should be."

> "What is the quality of your awareness? It's your
> degree of presence in the moment. This is your chance
> for real happiness, contentment, and peace."
> – Eckhart Tolle

So, tell me what "living in the moment" means to you. What are your thoughts on this? Do you understand present-moment awareness intellectually, but are not yet sure how to *live* in this state, or how to apply this philosophy? Well, consider your morning routine, for example. While you are brushing your teeth, I'm sure you are not thinking about "brushing your teeth," or "potential cavities," or anything like that. Instead, you are probably more focused on the day ahead. Are you worried about your job? Or do you have stress surrounding a test or exam you are about to take?

STEPPING STONE: Try this "in the moment" exercise: Start by choosing any mundane, everyday task, such as ironing a shirt, for example. Now instead of contemplating your day ahead while doing the ironing, actually watch your hand reaching for the iron. Then observe the iron coming in contact with your shirt. Watch your hand as it grips a little more firmly to the iron, and listen to the sound the iron makes as it slides back and forth across the material that is your shirt. Notice the steam emanating from the iron, but don't "think" about all this. Just observe the action of ironing your shirt, and do so with no thought involved. Try this same exercise when you brew your morning coffee, or pour yourself a glass of juice from the fridge. You can even perform this exercise when you pop a waffle into the toaster, or when making your favorite smoothie.

You can also try *this* exercise: Raise your right hand so to view the back of it. Now with your left index finger, begin slowly tracing the outline of your fingers on your right hand. Observe the shape and condition of your hand…its lines, veins, grooves, and wrinkles. Notice the condition of your nails and cuticles. Stop for a moment to see if you can actually feel the energy emanating from the center of your palm—your palms being one of the most vital meridians within the human body. If you're doing this exercise correctly and without judgment, you should be totally immersed with the look, feel, and energy of your right hand, without having any thoughts as to the events and/or circumstances of your day.

The goal here is to learn to be totally in the moment through the act of simple observation. If you are truly focused on the task at hand, then there is no stress. After a minute or so of thoughtless and effortless observation, assess your stress level. How much anxiety did you have before this exercise, and how much did you have while in total presence and observance of your right hand? In doing this exercise, you probably had very little or no stress. And this means you were in the moment! Remember, fear (stress) is *time-based*. And where there is no time, there is no fear.

And now for one last question: If you were able to find presence during the prior exercise, did you feel peaceful in that moment?

Now apply this exercise to everything you do today. Start with your commute to work. During your drive or ride, make simple observations of your surroundings without considering your day ahead. Your issues won't disappear, but the anxiety related to them will. Once you master this practice, your fears will be greatly reduced or eliminated. And this reduction in fear will open a creative space from which you can allow inventive ideas to germinate. You will be in a position to receive all of the goodness you desire because your limiting thoughts will be, well…limited! You will become an "allowing machine."

Your new process when challenged:

From this point forward, when facing a challenging moment, I want you to practice this process:

- Feel the negative thought or energy coming toward you
- Heighten your awareness around what may be coming

- Breathe deeply
- Immediately think: *peace and space*
- Make a commitment to *participate* in the moment
- Become aware of your emotions, remain emotionally healthy
- Take the edge off —"Everything is as it should be"
- Remember, every situation is a learning opportunity
- Breathe deeply
- Remain poised and graceful
- Determine you are going to help this person (resolve this situation, etc.)
- Keep your wellbeing in mind
- Listen and display infinite patience
- Feel the creative space between you and the issue
- Remain decluttered and non-judgmental
- Now, just observe
- Feel the positive momentum building
- Be imaginative with your listening skills and possible solutions
- Just be happy
- Love and create
- Respond compassionately

Put yourself in this practice scenario: Your boss pulls you aside regarding your so-called "poor performance." Internally, you know you are on solid ground, because he is misinformed regarding the situation. Normally, you might knee-jerk react, or allow your blood to start boiling. In that moment, however, you decide to simply allow your boss to verbally blitz you, while your conscious awareness of the situation keeps your emotions in check. Since you are not in a twist, you are able to remain in a positive state, crafting creatively how you are going to respond—not defensively, but *gracefully*.

Now let' try *this* practice scenario: Your romantic partner tells you he's leaving work and is heading for home. But for reasons beyond his control, he arrives home 35 minutes later than originally anticipated. Normally, yourself to get into a twist in this type of situation, but this time you are standing up for your wellbeing by exercising a calmer, more open stance. Regardless of the reason he is late, you get to choose how you are going to feel about it. So why not choose "another plate of lentils?"

Here's the alternative: Let us say you *don't* handle the situation with grace and calm. Maybe you go off on him (enter the expletives here) when he arrives home. In this moment, you have chosen "selur's" way of handling things over Quality of Life. And now you have put your partner in a position of having to elevate *his* own awareness, so he can remain in a creative, loving space, because his wellbeing is important to him (just as yours' is important to you). And by putting "selur" in charge, what you're really doing is asking your partner to defend himself. And now there's a fork in the road. So what does he do? Well, maybe he battles back. Who knows? But really, only one of three things can happen in this scenario: (1) neither of you evolve in this moment, and you spend a miserable, angry evening together (2) only one of you evolves, or (3) perhaps both of you can grow together as spiritual beings, by exercising infinite patience and love, combined with participatory awareness

So you see, you Keep to Your Spiritual Path by remaining in a constant state of elevated awareness regarding how you are feeling, all the while choosing whether you are going to habitually react, or calmly respond, to your life's circumstances. It also helps to apply moment-to-moment mantras (coming up!) to help keep you grounded on your Path. As your conscious awareness becomes continually heightened, this way of living will eventually become second nature, and you will feel more peaceful with each passing day.

Put yourself first in line!

During life's so-called "challenging times," you should double your efforts and become even more self-aware, so as to continually look within, as a reminder to Love yourself deeply. This is a very important and profound lesson we all need to remember. It's so easy to let daily life wear us down, at which time we usually put ourselves last in line, spending very little time on our own spiritual practice. And when we're worn down, this creates a more fertile environment for our low-energy thoughts to run wild, which then creates a fearful and paralyzing existence. And who wants that? Why do we allow this to happen?

Fortunately, we live in an ever-evolving Universe. And at some point, you will become self-aware, realizing why you have not found or kept to your spiritual Path. And this is a moment where you can practice acute awareness by focusing inward. Yes, along this journey you must learn to Love yourself. Build on this for a few moments. When was the last time you really looked at yourself in the mirror? And I don't mean to pop a zit, or to freak out because you have a new wrinkle or strand of gray hair. I'm talking about getting up close to the mirror, so you can look deeply—and consciously—into your own eyes.

If you have never done this, trying it will blow you away. Just allow yourself to have fun with this. At some point you will begin to smile because, initially, it's kinda weird. But as you allow your smile to coat your Being, walls begin to come down. In this moment, just say out loud, "I love you, I love you, I love you!" Say it to yourself at least 50 times or more. The most fantastic feeling will wash over you...the shackles of past self-doubt and guilt will break away. You will ask yourself why you have carried these burdens for so long.

You can't help anyone else until you begin taking care of your own wellbeing. This is why the flight attendants advise you to put on your own oxygen mask, prior to helping the person next to you. Well, living with a renewed sense of self-care falls under this same principle. So immerse yourself in a joyful place, and you will be able to give so much more than you currently do. Consider what makes you happy. For me, it's a bunny (yes, I'm a guy and I like bunnies, *okay?*). Or many times I imagine my favorite place in the world, which is a path along the forest's edge in the German town where I've spent much of my life.

So what can you think of which will immediately make you smile, or allow you to feel the energy of Love emanating throughout your Being? Go there now in your mind, and allow yourself to smile from within. Let that feeling linger for a minute. Allow it to cleanse your mind of all things. *Begin to feel the power of Love flowing through you!*

So by now you're probably wondering what it is about a bunny that makes me feel so good? Well, a few years back when I would come home after a long, and sometimes trying, day, I see our two rabbits, Bunny and Sadie, hopping around the backyard. Blissfully eating dandelions and clover, they then see me, and motion for me to come over to give them some Love. I mean, what's more adorable than that? That is one place I visit in my mind when I need to be reminded of living in a more peaceful, joyous, and Loving state. And why not live in this state at all times? Today, our cat, Lucy, provides that same cleansing effect. We're convinced she allows us to live in her house. She runs the place with her own brand of cat manipulation and adorableness. Remember, you create your own reality...and the emotional state in which you reside is your choice.

When you decide not to be bothered by something, you are growing and taking another step down your Path. And it's from this creative space that you are able to calmly solve your issues, and move forward into a healthier state of Being. As you feel the weight of problematic thinking lift from your heart and shoulders, you will start to feel better, and your conditions will begin to improve. Remember, stand up for your wellbeing! And keep in mind there's a big difference in "not letting something bother you" versus "blowing things off." In the former, you are detaching from negative emotions, while allowing the space of awareness to help you engender a positive solution. Blowing something off, on the other hand, is a dysfunctional avoidance tactic fueled by "selur," and this doesn't fix the problem. In fact, the avoidance of issues that need to be faced and dealt with could cause things to deteriorate even further.

Ultimately, when you choose to participate in life, you then have total control over your wellbeing. And when you combine this approach with a flexible mindset—by remaining open yet discerning to the thoughts and opinions of others—you will bypass judgment, eliminate turbulence, thereby setting the stage for experiencing a wonderful moment. Learn to connect special moments, one after another, and you will live a more peaceful, meaningful, and abundant life...and that is what life *is*: a string of beautiful moments just waiting to happen.

Keeping to Your Spiritual Path by aligning with goodness:
"But where do I start?" you ask. "And how do I overcome myself?" you plead!

These are questions I know many of you have. And I believe the problems many people experience are not being solved by the outdated model in which one goes through a long, drawn-out process that can cost a small fortune. Many people certainly appreciate being pointed in the right direction, but most make the process too complicated.

The healthy journey is one of perspective. When you release the tight grip you have on your negative emotions, a new day will dawn for you. When you focus on your new story of today, leaving the worries of tomorrow behind is a simple thing. When you do nice things for yourself and others, emitting Love all day long, you leave little room to consider a painful past or the stress of tomorrow. Yes, this conscious way of living requires study and practice, but if your perspective is one of curiosity, you will shed the negative energy and feel much better immediately.

So far, I've talked a lot about "the Path" in this book, and why we all need to keep to it. And now is the time to dive into the principles you can apply today. Beginning *now* (not on Monday), you will be able to make instant adjustments to your life, which will help you to Keep to Your Spiritual Path. I have listed some of these adjustments in the following text, and will talk about each one in greater detail. Just remember that the key here is to *open your mind to these ideas, to allow for the immediate and nurturing impact they may have on you.* You may be in your spiritual infancy, so it's very important to your reconditioning process that you allow the goodness of these simple concepts to pervade. *Close the chasm by applying the goodness...which follows*:

I ask you now to allow yourself to become a little more vulnerable. Because when you are vulnerable, you are in a trusting state of mind. Be open and allow for the presence of new, healthy information to enter your psyche. *"Trust," in this case, means to disregard any limiting thoughts or feelings of discomfort you might have related to the following concepts.* Don't make a big deal out of it, just allow the process to unfold. This is an easy method of implementing basic ideas compressed in a new way. You can apply them at your own pace. And this will work well for you if you trust in the process.

It is now time for you to learn how to lay metaphorical bricks along your Path. These bricks are to become special for you, so embrace them beyond face value. In order to truly Keep to Your Spiritual Path, you should consider them, and incorporate them into your daily practice and newly acquired belief system. No longer taking these everyday offerings for granted, your investment in them will tip the scales in your favor. Your mission is to consciously practice the philosophies associated with each brick, and to do so with deliberate intent. No more just "going through the motions" of life. *You will become aware now and focus on the bricks below.* After that, we will delve deeper into defining your daily practice.

Beginning *today*, believe in the *Why?* associated with these bricks:

- Nature
- Flexible mindset
- Shifting the way you think
- Non-judgment
- Releasing controlling behaviors
- Offering gratitude
- Generosity
- Slowing your pace
- Tell a new story

The aggregate of these principles is the genesis of the new you. This process goes back to the idea of cleansing your Being, reconditioning your thought patterns, and applying the power of Love to everything you do. Once you genuinely have harnessed and mastered laying these bricks, day by glorious day, you will feel your life gel in such a manner that Love becomes the predominant force in your life. You will vault (as I said earlier) toward creating the best "you" possible.

Be intentional

Brick of Nature

Begin here. Go to the woods, lake, ocean, or just look at the plant on your desk. If you're choosing the houseplant, observe it for several minutes, noticing its simplicity and perpetual balance. Allow yourself to become peaceful in this moment. From this space, understand that it is okay for you to shift inward toward spirituality, and to walk its Path. Feel within your very Being that you are open to awakening to what you already know. Your soul wants a little breathing space... it just wants to emerge. So give back to it by growing internally and shedding the undesired. You will know innately what to do while you blossom and unfold; trust your instincts. Nature will ease you into it. Trust Nature and it's purity of form. It provides. It gives.

When you wake up each morning, make it a priority to appreciate the splendor of the rising sun. Stop for a moment and take a few deep breaths, as the sun gently warms your face. Every person should begin his/her day this way. Give thanks to the sun for all it does for our planet. Find a way to step onto a patch of grass today. Some of you never even tread on the Earth—or at least you don't do so consciously, and while in your bare feet! Stand upon the Earth, and feel the awesomeness of the true Mother. Connect with this precious gift we have been given. Do your part to respect Her and to give back to Her in any way possible. When you allow it, Nature's peace is inescapable. So observe Nature's simplicity, and feel yourself becoming more abundant. God is everywhere. In those moments when you feel so deeply in touch with Nature, your connection to God is wide open. This is why Nature feels so good!

I wrote earlier about the effortless decluttering of the mind, and how Nature can assist you in achieving this state. Well, what did you learn from that teaching? From Day One, you can learn to appreciate a maple tree outside your office window, or a picture of a glimmering lake on your calendar. Allow yourself to soak in a few seconds or more of what these images *provide* you. Sense the miracle of life. See the purity of a snowflake gently dancing earthward. Acknowledge

Nature's perfect balance. Let Nature's abundance be the symbol of all that you have, and of all that you want to be.

Be in the moment. Don't think so much about the flower's beauty...just observe it. Begin then to relate to its lifestyle; it just "is." Try emulating Nature's composure, and see how your life might shift in this regard. Remain steady at all times. Choose a vision or a place in the natural world you have previously visited, and go there in your mind during troubling times.

When I am peaceful and in a state of gratitude, I put up fewer or no barriers to the imminent desires I want to have come my way. Nature keeps me to my Path by helping me focus on this peaceful and gracious state of mind. And this, my friends, is when my desires are realized. The treasure Nature offers me is legit balance in my daily life. And it is this balance that opens my mind, setting the stage for greater flexibility.

Brick of Flexibility

Inspired by Nature, begin your spiritual practice with the requisite concept that is "flexibility." Without it, you will remain who you are, entrenched in your current dire circumstances. Flexibility and awareness work hand-in-hand. When you are open to new ideas, your life will flower. You may not understand or apply these new ideas right away, but you will reduce the amount of turbulence in your mind by not immediately rejecting concepts, which are currently not part of your daily life or thinking patterns.

I, personally, want to remain flexible and open to the issues at hand, and to bend with them. That's not to say I wilt or "give in." It means I don't become rigid, thereby creating turbulence in my mind, or in my heart. The openness I exhibit allows me to remain inventive and solution-oriented. It keeps me peaceful and emotionally balanced.

Reducing the turbulence in your mind is a fundamental practice you will need to employ—and I will continue to address this issue throughout the remainder of the book. You see, with a flexible mind, you don't immediately judge circumstances. Your mind becomes more relaxed and imaginative. And this way of Being takes the pressure off. A flexible attitude permits you see the world with your chin up, instead of down, as you walk along life's road.

Look at it this way: In order for you to develop as a person, allow walls to fall so you can objectively disseminate new information. This creates new opportunities of all kinds.

Flexibility is also a precursor to stillness. In peace and quiet, you are able to connect with God and manifest your dreams. In the end, the Universe will present itself to you in ways you currently cannot comprehend. There are also other dimensions you may potentially explore. There are quantum-level depths yet to be discovered by most people.

It's important to know that the real opportunities in life reside in "uncertainty." What I mean to say is, you may only feel safe in what you currently know, while being petrified by the idea of change. But the reality is, life changes constantly all around us. So if you struggle against change, you will lose your momentum and remain stagnant. But here's the irony of it all: There actually is no safety in your control and rigidity. There is no safety in your unwillingness to change.

Lao Tzu says when you are rigid in your thinking, you are like a dead tree. And in this way, you consort with death. Yet when you are flexible, like a young sapling, you harmonize with life. With which do you consort? Life or death? Rigidity or flexibility?

While I was living in Germany years ago, a radio report spoke of a huge windstorm, which was set to roll through our region during the following day. News reports advised us all to refrain from entering the woods, because the falling of trees and branches was imminent. It was mid-autumn, and quite dry outside. As soon as I heard the report, I immediately knew I was going into the woods the next day! Now I don't condone what I did, but I just couldn't contain my excitement, because I love big storms of all kinds!

The next morning, the sun was shining and, sure enough, it was quite blustery outside—the powerful broom of Nature was sweeping away the dust and debris. I waited, though, for the real wind to arrive before I entered the woods backing to my home at the time. So around 11:00 a.m., my mind brimming with, *What cool stuff is about to happen?* I entered the trail. Within seconds, I heard the wind ripping through the canopy. Trees were bending and leaning on each other for support. My head was on a swivel, as I walked forward, slowing spinning in circles, trying to see each tree possible. I knew I had to be one step ahead of each falling tree and branch.

I was about a half-mile down the trail when I heard the first big CRACK of a branch snapping behind me. Even though it was far enough away, it forced me to look up. It was both exhilarating and scary. I was smiling nervously ear to ear. I continued to keep my eyes and ears peeled for falling trees. I was encircled by danger. Then, as I looked about 100 yards down the trail, a huge gust blasted through the trees, sweeping the abundant, brown leaves lying on the ground high into the air, creating a 20-foot-tall cyclone of fallen debris. So exciting! The sustained gust tilted the tall trees, bending their tips so far over I thought they were going to touch the ground. I was blown away—*literally!*—by their majestic flexibility.

Needless to say, I made it safely out of the woods that day. Because of that experience, though, I felt full of life and totally present in the moment. My slightly irresponsible decision led to one of the most exciting moments of my life. Deep down, I knew I would come out of those woods just fine, even though I was going into them during cyclone-like conditions. I had that conviction! The next day the local newspaper reported the storm. They took statements from people who recounted the various ways in which they took to safety and protection. I smiled to myself, wondering what I may have said had the local news interviewed *me!* The report also advised people not to enter the woods for a few days so broken branches and weakened trees would have a chance to fall or settle. So what do you think I did...?

While walking your Path, you will be presented with challenges. In those moments, think about something that represents flexibility in your mind. I always think back to the bending trees on that dry autumn day. The trees taught me how to be infinitely flexible. When those challenges are at your doorstep, don't think about what you may lose...instead, consider what you will gain.

I knew I would be okay on that day, and that I would have a fantastic time. I was uncertain of exactly what would happen, or what I might experience, but I was excited for the opportunity. I exited the woods in perfect health, and with a new experience (and metaphorical teaching!) under my belt.

Do you live in fear of what you don't know? Do you like the way fear makes you feel? Probably not. As difficult as this may sound, experiment with introducing a little flexibility into your life. Remember, fear needs more fear to exist. Don't feed "selur." Open your mind to something new. What's the worst that can happen? Flexibility offers you the opportunity to create the life you want. It is that easy.

"A foolish consistency is the hobgoblin of little minds."
– Ralph Waldo Emerson

What Ralph is saying here is that stubborn rigidity is the sign of a small thinker. How can you steadfastly maintain an outdated way of thinking when new data proves otherwise? Just because you have maintained a certain opinion for a long period of time ("My daddy always told me..."), this doesn't mean you can't change your mind, opening up your stance to a different point of view. Flexibility in mind and point of view is a sign of growth.

Flexibility is a cornerstone in your reconditioning process, and leads to shifting how you think.

Brick of Shifting

With your rediscovered flexible mind, you are now open to shifting the way you currently process circumstances. Since you want to improve the conditions of your life, you have to grasp and commit to the idea that you must change your perception of the information flowing to you. For many people, change is challenging. So don't try to "change"! Simply "shift" a little bit. Rule Number One is to become more aware of your thoughts. Remember to keep a flexible mind and to be open to new concepts. Understand you don't need to make immediate sweeping changes in your life. Simply accept the idea of *slightly* shifting the way you think.

Terrified of change? I understand that. If, though, there are aspects of your life you wish to be different, take the "shifting" approach. Just make a slight move in your life by allowing in a little daylight. If it feels right, shift a little more. And then keep shifting until you have arrived at a place where things become easier. Remember, the only constant in life is change. Learn to become comfortable with shifting and you will lead a much happier life. An example of shifting is the mere willingness to implement some of the philosophies within this new belief system.

Be true to yourself by following through on what you know to be honest and healthy. In other words, stop telling yourself "someday." Stop saying, "I really should..." If you know you "should" do something, do it! Start with small tasks, like cleaning out your filthy car, or finally taking the Christmas lights off the house (in July!). *Should* you play more with your kids? Then do it! *Should* you put in a little more effort at work? Then do it! *Should* you stop using the carpool lane as a solo driver? Get a grip!

Personally, when I shifted and began keeping the promises I made to myself, something clicked inside of me. I feel as if I can accomplish anything now! This has been the easiest change I've made in my spiritual life. Do this!

Live this way for a month. You will be amazed how this simple shift in your life can make you feel so clean. Try it and tell me how it impacts you.

STEPPING STONE: It's time to shift from fear to curiosity. Consider for a moment the stress and anxiety your fears cause you. Feel the dramatic impact they have on your mental and physical wellbeing. Are you tired of how your fears make you feel? Have you had enough of it? Well, it's time to cure that once and for all.

Right now, take a current fear and think about it for a few

seconds…how does it instantly make you feel? Does your belly twist and hurt? How deep does the pain run? Think about it a little more…

Assign your fear and/or pain a score of one through five, with five being the most painful. Now with an open mind, you are going to assign it the *new perspective of delightful curiosity.* Breathe in deeply… once again… slowly open your mind. Now, look at this fear, *not* as it's interwoven throughout your Being, but as a small white cloud floating overhead. Observe it like you would a rainbow. What do you feel when you first see a rainbow across the horizon? Elements of wonder and curiosity always seem to bubble to the surface. Maybe you smile. How do the colors form? What makes them so intense? How does a double rainbow materialize? Fantasize about the gold! Let it sink in…

Now shift and look at your small white cloud of fear with the same fascination. Detach yourself from what your white cloud represents. Remain in a state of wonder. Simply tilt your head and become curious about this fear…this little white cloud. Let the curiosity sink in. Do not attach yourself to the white cloud. Keep it overhead. Ask yourself: *What is the value of this fear? Do I need it?* Without relating to the past negative feelings it's always given you, ask yourself what value it really has for you. Just remain curious…remain curious… stay tilted…remain curious…stay there for a moment…

If it helps you further, go back and do the exercise again with a little more focus. Sink yourself into it. Allow your curiosity to be the catalyst that melts away the anxiety.

Did you have some success? What are your emotions now, related to this fear? Has your new delightful perception of this fear turned to daylight? Do you feel less impacted by the fear? Is your white cloud evaporating? What score do you give it now? Cool, huh?

The value of this exercise is not so much in answering the questions, but in remaining curious and seeing your white cloud from a new and healthier perspective. You see, curiosity is an "in the moment" concept. So where there is no time, there is no fear.

Shift from fear to curiosity and feel the weight lift. Participate in each moment through heightened awareness, and feel your life open to all possibilities.

Take a little peak around the corner of opportunity; consider a shift you'd like to make. For example, are you thinking of beginning a meditation practice? If so, be open to its benefits. Be amenable to allowing yourself the 20 minutes of "me" time each morning. Be open to researching more about how to do it. Become comfortable talking about meditation with others. Remember, it doesn't matter what other people think...just be yourself. Some people find it easier to attend a guided group meditation. So go out and find the meditation group or practice that works best for you!

Then, when it feels more comfortable, shift a little more. As you find comfort in this process, you will begin shifting in other areas of your life with more ease and grace. It will become less challenging each and every day. And soon, your development and growth along your Path will become quite evident. You will notice a remarkable difference in how you feel, how you handle situations, and how you view your life and its possibilities. People will tell you that you are less stressed and that you are emanating positive energy (although they may say this in their own words!). You will also hear that you have a calming effect on those around you. You will radiate peace without even realizing it. You will become contagious—in a good way!

After some time, take another emotional inventory, and see where you stand in comparison to 36 or even 68 days ago (these are arbitrary numbers!). Soon it will become apparent to you that "shifting" is much easier than attempting to "make big changes all at once." This way, Keeping to Your Spiritual Path can be a more tranquil process. Conversely, if you try to change your life immediately, all at once, you most likely will stub your toe along the way. Just like with suddenly dropping a large amount of weight through an unhealthy crash diet, you are more likely to gain it all right back now, aren't you? So put in the time necessary to make small, subtle shifts in the way you walk your Path, and you will wake up one day feeling wonderful. You will be well on your way to recognizing your dharma!

Shifting leads to all kinds of possibilities, awakenings, and epiphanies. There is no better feeling you can attain than to feel the joy of liberation, and a deep connection to God, your Source.

You feel in that connective moment the presence of your purpose. And through this connectedness, you will see the obvious design by which we are all meant to live. There is only goodness…only Love is real. And when you start to "get" this, you will see the stark contrast in the world around you. You'll want to scream to the naysayers: "STOP DOING WHAT YOU ARE DOING! NONE OF THOSE LABELS MATTER! COME WITH ME ON THIS JOURNEY! JUST LOVE ONE ANOTHER, HELP EACH OTHER, AND JUST 'BE'!"

Shift slightly each day, and you will fall into the gap of infinite possibilities. Healthy shifting combined with flexibility allows you to reduce and/or eliminate the turbulence caused by a judgmental attitude, and an over-cluttered mind.

Brick of Non-Judgment

The greatest accelerant to emotional freedom you can employ is the elimination of judgment. When you combine non-judgment with total awareness, you will be well on your way to enlightenment.

Judgment is at the top of "selur's" food chain, because judgment is a form of fear. People judge other people, and their situations, all day, every day of their lives. Each time one judges, a kind of turbulence is created within the mind and, through the Law of Attraction, one will bring that which is judged upon one's self. This is not a good thing.

If you judge someone, you are saying that person is wrong and you are right. And in doing so, you are placing yourself above that person, which is a deviation from your spiritual Path. This must cease in order for you to attain the life you desire.

The truth is, you are no better or worse than any other soul on this planet. No, you are not superior to the transient woman living on the streets. And a cardiologist who saves lives is no better than a housepainter. Labels and layers don't give you the right to judge anyone or anything. Every time you judge or speak harshly about someone, you bring that like vibration onto yourself. Know this truth.

Recall I spoke earlier of not allowing life's conditions to impose its will on you, thereby dictating how you feel. Well, this works both ways—meaning you cannot live from your soul's perspective while simultaneously judging, and therefore imposing your narrow way of thinking on someone else's condition. Your soul does not judge; that's "selur's" job. Tame it now!

One day, I was sitting in my car at the park. As I gazed out onto the park's landscape, I noticed two young men, about 18 years of age, walking across the grassy field. Because of their age, how they were dressed, and their overall demeanor, I unfortunately labeled them as "punks." I thought to myself, *Why are they not in school? They look like trouble.* But by judging them without having any real knowledge of their lives, I created turbulence in my mind, and within my own energy field. And since I placed a negative label on them (*There walk two punks.*), I created a strong negative vibration both for myself, and toward the young men as well. Lost went the opportunity to feel a loving connection.

However, since I was conscious of my spiritual development, my heightened awareness allowed me to immediately recognize my judgment of the two young men—so I quickly modified my thoughts to, *They're behaving like punks.* This is a very powerful shift in thinking, since I put the emphasis on their behavior, as opposed to the quality of their very Being. My shift in thinking, therefore, allowed me to recognize their beautiful souls, and that they were only acting from "selur" (just as I had previously done through my judgment of them!). Better yet, I could even think, *I see two beautiful souls who are learning how to shed their layers.* Now there is zero judgment on my part, hence a reduction in energetic turbulence, and the sprouting of a more conscious, beautiful moment.

The key here is to recognize, as soon as possible, when you take a step back, as shown in this example of what judging and labeling looks like. But just like I demonstrated, you can quickly recover by shifting your thinking, and sending a loving message to the Universe. *Those two men are taking a relaxing walk through the park just as I sometimes do. I wish them a wonderful morning.*

Reduce energetic turbulence by opening your flexible mind

to the idea of non-judgment. Let people have their opinions, their behaviors, and their own Paths in life. This is not an easy thing to do right away, but through your conscious awareness you will begin catching yourself more often. When you begin your practice of non-judgment, you will be stunned by how often you catch yourself placing accusations on the outside world. And the more you practice this kind of awareness, the better you will feel. This will eventually become second nature to you. The immediate result is the minimization of low-energy clutter trying to enter your precious mind. Stop the cycle! A mind free of clutter is fearless, imaginative, and resourceful.

Non-judgment creates space in your mind to contemplate gratitude, doing something special for someone, opening your eyes to the surrounding miracles, and nurturing your connection with God. Practice non-judgment and allow beauty to flow into your life. You will better recognize your purpose in life this way.

Practicing non-judgment represents a massive step forward, which puts you in a position to live from your soul's perspective. When you reduce and ultimately eliminate judgment, you open yourself up to boundless opportunities.

If you are thinking about beginning a meditation practice, your new non-judgmental approach will pay huge dividends. Meditation is a place where we rest our minds. In this state of repose, answers are provided to us. If you want to maximize your experience, you have to enter the meditation state with a decluttered mind. Non-judgment will help immensely for this purpose.

Another influential teacher of mine is Dr. Wayne Dyer. I never met the man, but his teachings have impacted me deeply. His book, *Change Your Thoughts, Change Your Life* does a masterful job in teaching non-judgment. I highly recommend the audio version because his spoken work has a way of resonating with people at a much deeper level. I listen to him often in my car.

Improve your life today by moving away from judgment. Also, be honest with yourself; don't judge in silence. Feel the relief…

After practicing non-judgment for quite some time now, I

can tell you my mind is much clearer and calmer. I feel free to live emotionally well. Without a doubt, my entire world is brighter and more joyful because the energy previously dedicated to judgment is now channeled into Love.

Brick of Releasing

Would you like to declutter your mind? Well then, respect your wellbeing by releasing your need to have the last word, to be right, to make your point, and/or obsessively control a particular situation or person. This type of need is not *loving* behavior. Any time you inflict your will upon someone else, you are creating turmoil in your mind. And remember, you attract that which you are. If you feel good about having the last word, you have just fed "selur" a bounty's feast. With every intention to control a situation, you set the hook of fear deeper into your psyche. When you attempt to force your will on someone or something, you are exhibiting a tidal wave of disrespect for both yourself and the other person. What makes you think your opinion is more important than anyone else's? And what gives you the right to act *that* way?

> "Why will you take by force what you may obtain by love?"
> – Powhatan

If you truly want a certain outcome to manifest in your life, use Love to attain it…don't use fear or controlling means. Relinquish this unhealthy behavior by respecting yourself and those around you so as to feel the quality of your wellbeing increase.

When you are open to other people's opinions and ideas, you don't feel the need to judge or object; so you, in turn, remain peaceful, creative, and loving. Simply respect the other person's point-of-view, and move through the conversation looking for win-win solutions and uplifting dialogue.

I understand releasing this behavior can be difficult. So if you're struggling with this idea, go back to "Belief Three" and read once again about how to abolish fear from your life. Freedom doesn't come from controlling people and situations. Freedom comes from letting go of this need and allowing others to have their own space. Everything is as it should be...

Brick of Gratitude

A mind inspired by Nature—open to change and free of judgment—creates more space for positive thinking. And that leads us to gratitude.

I can't say enough about giving thanks. And I'm not talking about politely saying "thank you" to your server at a restaurant, or the man who holds the door open for you. I'm talking about giving real, heartfelt, profound thanks for all that you have in your life. Once you realize the power of gratitude, you will truly begin to see the little miracles happening all around you.

Through an "attitude of gratitude" you will appreciate the air you breathe. You will rejoice in awaking each morning knowing you have yet another opportunity to learn and grow. You will give thanks because you have two legs with which to walk across your bedroom and into the bathroom—that you have soap in the shower with which to cleanse yourself, and a roof over your head that keeps you warm and dry. Begin with these basics, and then start focusing more gratitude on the state of your health and finances, as well as on the quality of the relationships you have in your life.

If you want to increase the level of heartfelt gratitude in your life, I recommend reading Rhonda Byrne's book, *The Magic*. Learn how to give and *feel* thanks for everything in your life regardless of how bad you think things are. Her book put into perspective for me the power of gratitude. Her wisdom points toward being grateful for what you have so you may receive more of it. But alas, if you don't give thanks for what you have, it will only be taken away from you. *Ouch!* In *The Magic*, Rhonda provides a simple, 28-day program, which will change your life.

You can begin immediately to attract more abundance into

your life by thanking the Universe for every penny you have. If you constantly think about how many dollars you *don't* have, then what you don't have will continue to show up for you. Be hyper-thrilled if you find a nickel on the ground, and thank the Universe for that symbol of abundance. Feel "rich" when you cash in a winning $1 lottery ticket. And from there, know that more will come. No more limiting beliefs for you!

I begin each morning by giving thanks. While still lying in bed, I thank the Universe for my great overall health, my emotional wellbeing, the strong relationships I have, my financial condition, etc. It doesn't matter if I have tons of money in my savings account, or if I have a negative balance. I still say "thank you" for the change in my pocket, and the money I know is coming to and through me soon.

I also give thanks for certain things in particular. For example, I may say, "Thank you for the positive outcome of today's meeting," or, "Thank you so much for this sunny, beautiful morning."

To turbocharge your gratitude, be sure to complete your "thanks" by saying *why* you are grateful! "Thank you so much for the positive outcome of my meeting later today because this will allow us to take the next step in the sale of the company."

This is important: Let us say you intellectually understand the Law of Attraction concept, and think you are appropriately applying it. But why don't the fruits of your labor provide you with your dreams-come-true? It is because you still have limiting beliefs. It could also be the result of a lingering negative thought pattern, which cancels out the manifestation of your desire. Take this lesson and go far beyond the intellectual. You must be profoundly grateful each time you say "*danke,*" "*gracias,*" and "thank you." By the way, merely going through the motions will never cut it. Just look in the mirror and determine if you are genuinely grateful for everything you have in your life. Smile with joy in your heart. Be deeply grateful for the smallest little details.

Practice real gratitude now. Live it, breathe it, and feel a shift happen.

Brick of Generosity

We live in a balanced Universe; balance is defined as equally opposing forces. This means giving is as important as receiving. In fact, they are one in the same. When you *give* unconditionally, you are also *receiving* the joy emanating from the person who's accepting your gift. If you also give that which you desire, the Law of Attraction states you will receive in like-kind. As an example, if you want more monetary abundance in your life, then give something representing that kind of financial gain to someone less fortunate.

If you have very little money to give, learn to give a small gift, a smile, a gesture, a prayer, a card, or your time. Give something of yourself every day…it doesn't have to be monetary in nature. Just make your gesture a special one by really going the extra mile. Instead of an email, for instance, pick up the phone and call your Mom or your best friend just to say, "Hi," and, "I love you."

I am extremely fortunate to have grown up in a generous family. If you think about it, much of who we are today is based upon our childhood experiences, and the connection we have with our nuclear families. As children, my sister and I were blessed to have spent much of our youth in Germany. And during this time, my Omi, Opi, Oma, and Opa would often gift us hundreds, and sometime thousands, of Deutsche Marks (the national German currency prior to the Euro). They always told us to save the money—*yeah, right!* We would spend it "wisely" as every child should…we bought toys, food, and cool European clothing. As we grew into our late teens and early 20s, our "savings" were spent on even *cooler* European clothing, dinners, travel, and…um…*bier.*

But my grandparents' generosity wasn't just financial. They also took us on tours of Europe, where I learned about other countries, people, food, and cultural contributions. I grew up with the understanding that we all, as humans, just want to be happy, but we all go about it a little differently. It was from my Opi, (my grandfather) that I learned about Nature and how to respect and appreciate it.

And these same lessons were applied to world history as we toured the region's castles and walked the vast grounds and gardens. From my Opa (my great-grandfather), I was taught how to be creative and give back to mankind. He helped many Jewish families escape Nazi Germany during World War II. My Omi (my grandmother) was always very balanced. She loved life…and it showed in her kitchen. From her I garnered my love of German cuisine, which spans from delicately prepared game dishes to simple desserts to tablescapes. My Omi also opened my eyes to trying foods from other countries. What better way to learn about a culture than through tantalizing your taste buds and filling your belly? Finally, from my Oma (my great-grandmother), I learned of peace, caring, and sweetness. She was a quiet soul, always content to smile, help others, and be in the moment. There was never a harsh word spoken from her.

My Mom, though, is the greatest giver I'm blessed to know. Her support is unwavering. Her love is totally unconditional in only the way a Mom can give it. (I love you, Mom!) My Dad also gave several great gifts to me: "Do it once and do it right, son." "Always be fair and honest." "Invest wisely" (haven't quite mastered that one yet). "If it doesn't impact you, don't worry about it." So from the bottom of my heart, thank you, Dad.

My sister, Joie, is the most unique person I know. Of all the people in my life, she stands up for her wellbeing unlike any other person I've ever met. She doesn't allow much to bother her at all and, if something does trip her up, she moves quickly through it so she can cleanse and, once again, return to her peaceful state of mind. It's the steadiness with which she lives that has been a real model for me. Where I tend to operate with loose guidelines, Joie's discipline, composure, and balance has become my rock. The bond we share is deep and profound. I can't imagine a life without her. *Danke*, Joie!

But there is one more person I must note here: His name was Herbert Kaufmann. I don't know why, but we called him Onkel Jacob (I need to check into that!), and he was a dear family friend. He was always jovial, always a prankster, always generous. He owned a local flour mill six miles from our home in Germany. Other than eating fatty, grilled pork, one of his greatest joys in life was stopping by the store every few weeks to load up on goodies. He used to throw down the top of his cream-colored Mercedes, and travel the countryside visiting friends and family unannounced. He would swing by, dropping off wine, sausage, chocolate, magazines, hugs, and kisses.

When visiting our family home, he'd stay for about 10 minutes for some light-hearted conversation, to tell a quick semi-dirty joke, and then he'd whisk himself back to his convertible parked in our driveway. I used to love yelling, *"Aufwiedersehen!"* to him from the front stoop, as he joyfully waved back, his longish white hair blowing in the wind, as he accelerated full-throttle off to his next stop. He was a cyclone! But Onkel Jacob didn't just deliver treats, he delivered Love and joy.

So why am I telling you all about my family in this particular Brick of Generosity? Because it was through their unconditional generosity that I became who I am today. Many times we don't realize who we really are until later in life. And it's during those reflective moments that we can give our thanks to those who had the greatest influence on our young lives. And what better way to honor the gifts we are given by those closest to us, than to pass them onto our own families, friends, fellow humans, and animals.

Now I have two stories for you:

My closest friends and I try to get together at each other's homes every month or so for a great dinner and some fun. We all enjoy amazing each other with yet another fabulous meal. Well, during one of these particular dinners from years ago, I chose to do something special for two very dear buddies. At this time, I was still in my spiritual infancy, and was just learning how to give from a higher level of consciousness. So I decided to make a genuine effort in this regard, by giving to my dear friends something which meant a great deal to me.

I have been a collector of German *bier* glasses and *steins* for most of my life (and my friends know this about me). And the most precious *steins* I own were the first two with which I began my collection. They are commemorative *steins* from an annual festival (Heimatfest) held in the small German town where my mother was raised. Well, long story short, I chose these two *steins*—which had great sentimental meaning to me—to give to my closest friends. After a second or two of separation anxiety, I suddenly felt utter joy in my heart as I wrapped them in plain paper and placed them gently into a bag. In that moment, I was beginning to feel the power of true giving.

In the car on my way to the big dinner, I was genuinely excited to give my friends the precious *steins* from my collection. I knew it would shock them because, well…dudes don't usually give gifts to each other. Anyway, as I walked into my friend, Andrew's house, he shot me a curious glance when he saw the bag in my hand. Knowing me as he does, he just smiled, allowing me to play show-and-tell when I felt the time was right. When my other friend, Doug, showed up a few minutes later, we all cracked a beer and settled into the living room, where we were watching a football game by the fire. I had the bag of *steins* placed neatly at my feet. I first thought I'd wait until after dinner to present the gift…you know, to create more of a "highlight" moment." But since we all had full beers in our hands, I decided to go for it right then!

Now what you need to realize is that, at this particular point in time, I had known these two guys for almost 30 years. So I looked at them both and told them I had something I wanted to give them. But first I told them how much I loved them and how much I appreciated their friendship and brotherhood. And without saying another word, I gave each one of them a *stein* wrapped in the plain paper. The "joy that was my Being" as I handed over each package was higher than I can ever remember. It felt so wonderful to fully submit myself to this "giving" moment.

Doug opened his *stein* first with Andrew only a few seconds behind. Realizing the gift in their hands, was to connect to the emotional attachment I had to the *steins*. Needless to say, the experience was astonishing for both of them. The look on their faces was one of shock, surprise, and wonder. In that moment, I know they both felt blessed, loved, and appreciated.

And I realized in that moment that I began my collection with those two *steins* just so I could give them away to my friends someday. Doug tells me he uses his *stein* for tea every morning, while Andrew only likes to drink from his *stein* on special occasions. Anyone can give away stuff they don't want, but unless there is joy in the giving, there is no benefit to it. So why not give something away which is extraordinarily special to you, and reap the Love and abundance from the seeds you have sown.

And now for one more story:

About one year later, after I gave my buddies the *steins*, I was blessed to feel the joy of generosity once again. Being an avid sports fan, I am a Seattle Seahawks season-ticket holder. There was a pre-season game I couldn't attend, so I decided to go to the stadium and sell my tickets. On the way downtown I considered just giving away the tickets, but thought it would be fun to give away the proceeds instead. So I sold the tickets to a young out-of-town couple for face value: $100 total. The couple had driven to Seattle from Eastern Washington, in the hope of finding some tickets. They literally pulled up to the curb from their three-hour drive right to me! The young lady got out of her car, looked right at me, and said:

"Are you selling your tickets?"

"Yup! And the seats are in the Hawks Nest!" I replied.

And so the woman bought the tickets right there on the spot! Talk about *allowing* something to happen! The Law of Attraction was in full swing on that day for all three of us!

As I started walking back to my car, I decided to rely on my intuition to help me identify someone to surprise with the money. As you can imagine, I was getting all kinds of looks from the game-day masses, as I'm walking, bobbing, and weaving in the opposite direction of the flow of the crowd. "Dude, you are going the wrong way—the stadium is *that* direction!" But I kept my eyes peeled for the best fans to whom I would give the money. I had no real criteria in mind; I just felt I'd know when the time was right.

Finally, I saw a dad and his young son. The dad looked to be in his early-30s, and his son looked like he was in the fifth or sixth grade. As soon as I laid eyes on them, I knew they were the perfect match for the $100 that was now burning a hole in my pocket! So we were walking toward each other and, at about 15 feet apart, I reached in my pocket and said to the dad, "Hey there! Can I give you guys something?"

The dad justifiably shot me a suspicious glance, not sure what was going on.

"I just sold my tickets and I'm flush with cash. Here you go… maybe you can buy your son a hat or something."

And with that, I handed him the money with a big smile on my face—it felt amazing that I could somehow contribute to their fun for the day. Then the dad, with a stunned look on his face, said, "Really? Are you sure? Thank you!" He really didn't know what to do or say.

And so, with a feeling of joy in my heart, I kept marching on. But after about 10 paces or so, I felt the need to turn around.

As I glanced back while still walking, the dad was standing in the same spot with the money still in his hand, as if I had just given it to him. My gesture of generosity obviously had a huge impact on him. The son had the same stance as his dad. And for some reason, I felt even more joyful when I saw that. My gift must have had a greater effect on them than I originally anticipated. The vision of the two of them frozen in the moment caused my joy to compound! I'm sure they will both tell this surprising story forever. And maybe this even inspired them to give a little more to other souls in their own way, as they journey through their own lives.

Now beyond the giving and receiving, the reason I tell you these stories is because of the subsequent abundance I reaped after giving away something from the heart. Within hours of giving away the money: a new client became part of my business; I found out my paycheck was more than I expected; my neighbor came over to my house with baskets full of fruits and vegetables from his garden; and I also received a gift-card to a local restaurant. And yes, all of this abundance came to me by the next day!

This is a giving Universe, and you receive that which you are (as I have just clearly demonstrated in the prior example). If you choose to walk and give, you will receive more of the same. But if you think people, animals, or the environment are there just for your taking, you will always be poor. Takers will always want, but givers reap the gift of abundance. So why not increase your Quality of Life with a new, exciting story of how you attracted abundance into your life! Your new belief system creates a shift to a positive mindset. And your new positive thoughts will, in turn, result in a new and extraordinary life for you.

Wash away the stains of negativity by flooding yourself with optimistic energy. Soon there will be no room for your tired, old stories. You create your own reality by how you feel. Your thoughts will dictate your emotions and your subsequent feelings. You can't control what pops into your mind, but you can certainly determine the chain of thoughts which follow. Immediately shut down the negative momentum of "selur" by shifting to positivity through the gift of generosity.

Make a friendly gesture to a stranger and bask in the warmth you receive in return. How many times have you heard musicians say they derive their energy from the crowd? They play their music, the crowd cheers wildly, which enables the musicians to play with even more enthusiasm. And then the "giving and receiving" bounces back and forth all night between the crowd and the musicians...the musicians and the crowd. Imagine how much energy athletes receive from 68,000 passionate, screaming fans!

Well, this same concept applies to you and your life—to your own spiritual Path. So give a smile to someone today—see that person smile back, and receive the energy of a wonderful moment. Later that night you will recall how you bonded with a fellow human being, and how the two of you experienced a beautiful moment together. And the vibrations the two of you sent to the Universe will be returned back to you when the season is right.

The key to giving is to begin seeing yourself as a conduit of sorts. And this means you must learn how to allow goodness to flow *through* you, not just *to* you. In other words, as you receive joy and happiness, Keep to Your Path by letting the goodness flow from you on to the next person. If it flows to you and you simply hold onto it, you are actually robbing yourself of joy, and the same goes for the other person you could have passed the joy onto.

Show your generosity by emanating Love all day to everyone you encounter. Look for opportunities to connect with people, wishing them happiness, laughter, and joy. Don't pick and choose who you bless based on your previous beliefs. Don't judge who should receive your well-intended vibrations, and who should not. Remember, you are better than no one—we are all souls, connected to one another, and born from the same Creator. Yes, you may observe a person who is struggling with his or her own issues, but underneath all of that is a pure soul, full of Love, just like you. So smile at each person you see. Not everyone will smile in return, but you can still walk away knowing you sent a positive message to that person, and to the Universe as well. Strive to be compassionate in every situation. The smile you give may be just what that person needs in that moment (whether they know it or not!).

STEPPING STONE: I'd now like to demonstrate a simple way in which you can begin practicing generosity in your own life. I begin my mornings by giving thanks. Then, when I get to my office, the first beautiful task of my day is to handwrite a thoughtful card to a friend, client, or loved one. And I do this with true joy in my heart because I visualize my friend/client/loved one receiving unexpected Love via the U.S. mail. My energy instantly climbs when I pick up my pen. It feels so awesome to give unconditionally, expecting nothing in return.

So who is the first person you will write today? Consider making this ritual something special. Treat yourself to a very nice pen. Try it out. Make sure it feels great in your hand and confirm the ink flows just the way you like it. Then choose a fine-looking box of stationary. Better yet, have personalized stationary designed for you, which better represents your unique personality. On a recent visit to the Amalfi coast, we splurged on fine Italian stationary and greeting cards. With the receivers of my cards in mind, perusing the local paper shops was a complete joy! Shop owners continue to lovingly manufacture their paper onsite as they have for generations. It was such a treat to meet them, support them and to now spread their "vehicles of joy" across the globe!

So, spend some time learning how to write with finesse again. Our penmanship as a culture has deteriorated in the last 20 years or more, so practice, practice, practice! Take pride in the power of the written word.

Give thoughtful time to the content prior to writing your first specialized note. Know that a few well-worded sentences can have a large impact on the receiver; it's really the sentiment that counts. Your handwritten note can even be a simple "thank you" for the delicious dinner you enjoyed with a friend. Acknowledge the effort she made in the meal's preparation; compliment the table-setting, and the delicious taste of the organic feast she prepared. In the end, though, it's the shared company that should really be celebrated!

Finally, take care in addressing your envelope. Write out "Avenue" instead of abbreviating it—this will add an extra-special touch to show you care. Go to the post office and pick out stamps that fit the season or a certain mood. After all, your handwriting, stationary, and customized postage stamps are all part of the package. Now, as you place a stamp on the card, imagine the look on your friend's face when she receives it…instead of an "everyday" email! The surprise of your specialized card will make her entire day!

Be *that* person in other people's lives. Be the giver. This engenders a feeling of Love, causing the receiver to potentially emulate you. Imagine the domino effect you can have on the world around you! It's this type of giving that creates momentum, gelling together your spiritual foundation. And through this healthy perspective, you can feel the responses to your emotional-inventory questions improve daily. Give and receive with sheer Love and joy!

Brick of Pace

Think about how many times you prayed for something to occur, or asked the Universe for a particular desire. Have you wondered why it never manifested or why you haven't received a response? Well, the response did come, but you were probably just too busy to hear it. The answers we seek sometimes come in the form of a whisper...a subtle hint like the kiss of a butterfly. Since the answers you seek don't always make themselves hyper-obvious, learn to interpret these elusive messages. You can easily learn to do this by slowing down the pace of your life.

Have you ever considered the pace at which you live? What about all of the filler activities you perform, which would otherwise provide you with some peace or a little downtime? Cultures that have existed for 2,000 to 3,000 years find it much easier to slow down than do younger cultures (like the United States, for example). The older cultures have already gone through their developmental cycles and don't have the need to move forward through their days at a breakneck speed. Yes, these cultures learned much in their long existences. They spend their time simply fine-tuning their high Quality of Life (and many of their inhabitants live to be more than 100 years old!). They live to live, not to accumulate! The USA, on the other hand (which is not quite 250 years old), and other adolescent countries, are early in their existence, so there is an innate need in their underdeveloped consciousness to do, do, do, do, do! These civilizations are always striving, accomplishing, building, and outdoing. This is the natural progression of a culture.

Take a look again at the first two questions in the preceding paragraph. Seems like you blink and another week of your life has raced by. (It's Thursday *again!?*) How does that happen? The reason time flies so quickly is because of the amount of activity you generate in your life and, therefore, within your own mind. Maybe you're one of those people who says "yes" to everything. Maybe you have kids who keep you running to playdates, judo, piano, cheer practice, the mall, and sleepovers at their friends' houses. Or maybe you have simply overcommitted yourself when it comes to your friends, family, community, neighborhood, and career.

Well, if you would like to take a step closer to your desires, consider giving yourself a chance to attain them. You can do this by simply saying "no" to a few things, some of the time. Sure, you will hear some pushback from the ones you have been previously enabling, but that will soon disappear, as you continue to stand up for your own wellbeing. Before long, the complaints will die down, resulting in you being able to obtain the respected quiet time you seek. Apply this simple concept where you feel it's needed throughout your life, and take advantage of the productive time you have created to step closer to your desires.

Another chief time-sucker is the compulsive need for the "filler activities," which serve to occupy any possible free time you might have available in your life. You have hundreds of opportunities per day to just take a deep breath. But since your mind is crammed with 60,000 thoughts per day, how can you possibly enjoy a brief moment at a stop light when you use that instant to compulsively check your phone? Or to worry about something you can't control? Or to listen to gloomy news on your car radio?

We oftentimes imagine a life with more peace and meaning. And so it's important to know that you are in total control of each topic I just discussed. The examples above are just that...*examples*. Therefore, you will need to fill in your own "waste of time" activities, that you probably use to distract yourself from that which you don't want to face or deal with. The point is you can do less and *feel* more. Just say "no" on occasion. You don't have to be at every party. You don't have to check your phone every four-and-a-half minutes. Tell your kids to take the bus once a week to some of their many activities. Tell your community leaders you just can't give 10 hours per week anymore (and believe it or not, they will get along just fine with you on a reduced schedule or—*gasp!*—without you at all!).

If you really do imagine a more peaceful and meaningful life, then try something very simple: Stand up for your wellbeing and use those moments to take that deep breath, appreciate the beauty of Nature, or even to just rest and relax for a while. This is not hard to do once you allow a peaceful feeling to be a higher priority in your life—that is, higher than checking Instagram or your Facebook page for the ninth time today!

And speaking of social media and technology, what are your thoughts on how you balance its presence in your life? I believe technology is a wonderful tool that has given rise to great innovation, brought together diverse cultures, and has seen old friends reunite. I also believe, though, that where it has connected us electronically, there is now a *disconnection* on a community level. Technology has created the degeneration of social skills and of simple human interaction (especially in our young people). There is now a gulf between people that before did not exist. But a community can come together when there exists a common bond.

Living in the Seattle area, our Seahawks are a cultural phenomenon in an already football-frenzied region. Their success has galvanized the community in a beautiful way. Strangers high-five and hug one another after each win or points scored. People from all walks of life talk about the team while in line at the grocery store. We even have "Blue Friday" here in Seattle, when everyone wears their Seahawks gear in support of the team, and in support of the community as well. We are affectionately known by the players as "the 12s"—an ode to the "12th Man"—the crowd inside the stadium.

The beauty of this fan-base is that neighbors who otherwise may not speak over the hedge, are now experiencing the beauty of human interaction because of this common bond. And I believe we can all connect in this same way on a *spiritual* level, and can leverage the opportunity to attain this heightened togetherness as a species. Just imagine if we were all on the same page, high-fiving just because...

Many times we learn to slow down by emulating other people or cultures. Check out how Parisians live: Their living rooms are the cafes that line the streets of their downtown neighborhoods. They are intimately connected to the moment and the satisfaction of what real Quality of Life delivers. Or observe how a gentleman sits quietly on a park bench, perfectly content to be alone with his thoughts, while enveloped by the abundance of his surroundings.

Recapture your "tweener" time. Prioritize and hold precious your mini Quality of Life moments. You will immediate surprise yourself by how wonderful it is to have a little free time all to yourself!

All right! How does all of this feel to you? Are you moving in a new direction? Excellent! Coming up are some tools you can begin to use immediately to put yourself in a joyful frame of mind. You are knocking on joy's front door!

When you honestly incorporate these eight simple principles into your daily practice, your level of joy will increase exponentially. You will find your outlook on life to be completely awesome. You will have epiphanies more often, with each one elevating your enthusiasm for growth. You'll feel ever more magical as you are reaping the benefits of the shifts you have made. The result will be an easy-flowing new story to tell. What a great way to take yourself to the next level! So now it's time to infuse your life with vibrant energy by telling your new story!

Brick of Stories

The stories you tell are all the conversations you have with people, day in and day out. It is how you convey your life's circumstances. It is in large part the face you show the world, and the attitude you have toward life. It is the way you communicate with your co-workers, a flight attendant, a bank teller, etc. You let the world know *who* you are by *how* you are. Your days will sing when you treat each individual encounter with joyful purpose and respect.

When you make up your mind to live a more joyful life, regardless of your circumstances, you are giving yourself permission to feel good *now*. And that permission instantly gives you the juice you need to see life from a more beautiful perspective. You find yourself walking the trail when, suddenly, you come to a short spur, which leads to a vista overlooking the rest of your life. With joy blooming within as you approach the view, what potential do you see for your life ahead, as you stand there perusing the forest of possibilities?

From this vantage point, you can do anything you'd like. Whether you see many or just one opportunity, claim it (or them) as your own. Reach for it and wrap your arms around it. Make it your destiny. As Brendon Burchard likes to say, "Throw your 'Spear of

Purpose' far into the fields of the future." Then make it your mission each day, and in each moment, to strive for that opportunity. Then pull the spear from the ground and throw it out there again. Choose your "thing" and complete tasks which allow you to get one day closer to reaching your dream. Gone are the days of by-standing as everyone else is moving forward.

Formulating your new story of positivity and Love will play a huge role in creating your destiny. In "Belief Three" we talked about releasing your fear(s). If you have done this or are working toward eliminating your obstacles, you have put yourself in position to shift toward your new story. Fill the void left by a fear with the positive practice of Love. The energy shift you feel as joyful conversations mount will be contagious to yourself and those around you. There is no doubt you will feel a profound difference in your wellbeing when you shift from focusing on the negative aspects of life, to the vivacious, fun, and abundant possibilities each morning has to offer.

To develop your new story, consider the life you'd like to lead. Now grab hold of that picture and practice the steps you need to take in order to attain it. Even if you have a short-term goal such as summer travel, for instance, create a fun story surrounding it. The key is to allow your joy to surface while you visualize and plan your trip. For example, your daily story can revolve around:

- the excitement of booking your flight
- the exotic place you are visiting
- the beautiful climate of your destination
- the huge stash of cash you have saved up for the trip
- the increased intensity of your fitness program and how great you will feel
- the delicious food you will savor and enjoy
- the cool people you will see, meet, and hang out with
- the sporty clothes and gear you will purchase

Doesn't this sound like a conversation you'd like to have? And it's okay if you don't have anything exotic planned. You can tell your new story about the delicious dinner you are cooking tonight by: talking of your fun trip to the grocery store, visiting an upscale wine merchant, and swinging by your favorite bakery. Even if dinner consists of mac 'n' cheese from a box, have fun with it! It all comes down to pivoting to a brighter perspective on your view of the world and what you are accomplishing with your new belief system.

But wait! There's more! You can create as many new stories as you'd like. With each new honest story you tell, you will feel your *Why?* become a deeper belief that will mature over time. Your vibrant stories will morph into a way of life for you. You will find that, as you focus on positive storytelling, your outlook on life and its perceived challenges will be much less daunting. You will instead recognize the richness in every moment. You will become smitten with life again! You will look forward to each breath you take.

BELIEF EIGHT
Your Spiritual Garden Shed

Let's strip away the "can't" and get down to bedrock.

This is my favorite section! In "Belief Seven," I opened your eyes to the concepts (or "bricks," rather) by which you can lead a more enriched life. And here, in "Belief Eight," I'm offering you some additional "daily tools" you can use to supplement and support everything you previously learned. In fact, many of these new and introductory principles may become mainstays in your life. Having the belief in these "every moment" practices is paramount.

Some of the daily tools I'm about to introduce will work for you right away, and some may take more time. The idea, though, is to walk forward with an open mind so as to discover what works best for *you*. Once you have been awakened to spirituality and what it represents for yourself and mankind, your thirst for knowledge will become immediate and insatiable. And as you begin to practice and apply new beliefs to your ever-evolving life, you will soon reap the seeds you sow. The key is to recognize and acknowledge your growth in that moment. Be cognizant that your practice is bringing results!

By now, you have felt how heightening your awareness and applying your shifting has led to you noticing the miracles surrounding you daily; even the faintest of details can make you smile. And you're probably feeling a new spring in your step because you're now realizing you can better control your mind, emotions, and life outcomes. This may not yet have clicked for you completely, but feel content in knowing you are well on your way.

Your spiritual foundation will set itself in its own time. Bricks lead to building blocks, which are laid through experiencing awakenings and epiphanies. But it is your daily practice which is the mortar cementing it all together. Through a daily practice, you feel the momentum beginning to build. The key to walking a progressive spiritual Path is the reduction and ultimate elimination of limiting thoughts *and* remaining in the ever-present state of awareness.

So what are the tools in your spiritual garden shed that you can use to cultivate your Path, and subsequently keep it weed-free? Well, below is a list of the tools you may use to do just that! You can employ most of the methods below immediately. Others you will take on when the season is right. Just do what makes the most sense in your own heart, and what resonates at the deepest level for you, personally. And remember, the aggregation of shifting builds toward real change.

I placed these daily principles in a philosophical order, in terms of what works best from morning to evening. I practice all of these principles every day. Some of the themes I've already talked about, so they will be familiar to you.

Here are your daily tools!

Gratitude

In the morning when you awake, begin your day by giving thanks to the Universe for everything you have. Continue to do this often throughout the course of your day. Remember to give thanks with as much feeling as possible, and to also give the *reason* for your gratitude (thank you, Rhonda Byrne!). Beginning your day by giving thanks puts you in a loving state of mind. Give thanks for the soap you are about to use, the clean towels on the rack, and the water spouting from the showerhead. As you do this throughout your day, you will find fewer things to complain about.

Flexibility

Remind yourself throughout each day to remain flexible and open when a "perceived" negative situations arises. This is one of the most important concepts of this book, because if you are closed-minded, you will never reach your desires. Flexibility doesn't mean you agree with everyone on everything. It just means you are allowing someone to have his/her opinion so that no energetic turbulence or resistance can clutter the sanctity of your precious mind. Flexibility also allows you to be open to new ideas that you can apply to your life. Through flexibility, you may develop your own personal philosophies on how to move more progressively along your spiritual Path. Exciting stuff!

Truth

Back in the day, I used to sugarcoat situations in order to avoid conflict or uncomfortable moments. I thought this way of interacting was no big deal, because who was I really hurting, right? Well, I eventually found out that the opposite is true. Sugarcoating is a form of emotional dishonesty. So in the past, when I was glazing over the truth in an attempt to keep things "comfortable," I was, in actuality, hurting everyone involved, including myself. I learned many years ago that we are all responsible for our own feelings, our own Path, as well as our own unique life lessons. So if you have something to say, express yourself honestly, and allow the other person the opportunity to deal with the clean facts. Yes, we must all understand that there's an appropriate time and place to drop certain knowledge on people—of course, civility, tact, and common sense play a role in our daily communications with those around us. But the point is, just be honest and open. If you're one of those people who has a tendency to sugarcoat things, learning to express emotional honesty may be a little scary for you in the beginning. But know that, ultimately, this form of self-expression frees your mind, allowing for truthful conversations with unpolluted facts.

For example, if you are late in arriving to your sister's house for a dinner date, don't call and tell her you are 10 minutes away when, in truth, you still have another 25 minutes to go. The days of blaming it on "traffic" are over. She may not be happy, but it's the truth! (Better yet, learn to arrive at your engagements five minutes early.)

Be truthful to others and yourself—don't sully your reputation! Always remember the Law of Attraction is perpetually delivering to you what you emotionally emanate. So if you continually sugarcoat your truths (or flat-out lie about the way you are feeling), you will receive the same in return. But if you remain honest in your communications, you will be flooded with good truths and real information. When we all have honest information with which to work, we can all operate on an equal spiritual playing field.

Meditation

Along the course of my own spiritual Path, I've contemplated quite a bit on the pace of thought. For most people, thoughts run quickly in any given direction, many times repeating the same cycle day after day (much of the populous refers to this cognitive dysfunction as "racing thoughts"). I think this scattered way of thinking has become such a norm in our society because it requires no effort to be swept up by the rushing current of life. You need only to jump in and, before you know it, you are bobbing up and down trying to secure your bearings. You may be wearing the lifejacket of positive thinking to keep you from going under, but this is not always enough to get to calmer waters.

Before you know it, many years have passed, one day merging into the next, as your life remains in a state of "mediocre." Why do we allow this to happen? This fascinates me. Since we know the answers we seek lie within us, what can we do as people to promote looking within as a daily exercise? And what can we do so this practice becomes a part of everyone's life experience? For if one does not look within, nothing in life will change, and blame will always be dished. And the false sense of security the positive-thinking lifejacket provides will always dominate.

142

Since most people are determined "not to go under" in life, sure, they learn to acquire a few navigational skills. They still struggle in the rapids of life, though, occasionally colliding with a boulder along the way. But every so often they find a peaceful stretch, and use that to regain their strength. They eat kale for dinner and go to bed early, thinking they are set for the next set of rapids—all the while hoping that down-river will be a little calmer than the fury of yesterday.

But there is a better way, you know: When you can learn to slow your mind and work *with* the river, you learn to rotate to your back, surfing the waters with your feet leading the way. This method keeps your head up and your eyes open, as you anticipate the boulders and logs along the way.

And it is through stillness that you can eliminate the clash with your mind!

Stillness is the only way you will gain a measure of control over your mind and "selur." When you simply stop *everything* for a few minutes to do *nothing*, allowing real stillness to pervade, a sense of calm takes over. When you turn your attention inward and focus on your own wellbeing, you begin to spiritually realize what is of utmost importance in life: the peace and tranquility of your inner world, which represents the "true mind."

This is the key to closing the chasm between "almost" and YES! Which is why I want to use this section to open up the topic of meditation. You see, each meditation session disengages you further from "selur's" voice in your head. Because it is "selur's" deceitful tone that has you believing you are your ego. But each time you meditate or take time to be still, you increase your awareness of "selur's" voice, thus breaking free of its deceit yet again. And over time, your awareness takes the place of this voice, allowing your ego to lose its influence over you. The aggregate of a focused, daily meditation practice represents the ever-widening aura of Love. And it is the impenetrability of this beautiful aura that keeps negativity at bay, as you flourish and expand in all directions of your life experience.

Every person should begin their day with a moment of stillness before rushing out the door, and dealing with situations as they present themselves. When you are willing to give yourself that brief moment, you can then build on this practice throughout your day. Even if you just look out your window to the sky and take a few deep breaths, you can still feed your soul, giving it a chance to come to the surface. Better yet, carve out a 10-minute segment each morning for your "starter" meditation practice—and you will quickly find that everything you seek resides there in stillness. There, nothing is lacking…in fact, everything is present.

> "Be still and know that I am God."
> – Psalm 46:10

In the Bible it says: "Be still and know that I am God." When you read that, what does it mean to you? Once you go beyond the words, at some point you arrive at: "When you slow your mind, you will hear Me." Of course, you will have your own interpretation of what you will "hear." But I believe this means that, in order to truly hear God, you must be willing to be still, releasing your connection to the physical, emotional, and mental world, so you can completely *connect to and hear* God's whisper.

You will accomplish this in your own way. Perhaps you have a comfortable chair facing your favorite picture window. Or maybe you have a spot in your garden you have created just for the purpose of relaxation. I'm sure there are many of you who like to go to the beach to stare at the horizon. And there are also those of you who unwind by going for a leisurely walk or a vigorous run. For me, connection and listening are best accomplished through meditation and thoughtless observation. Being still also means you are willing to release "selur's" grip on your psyche, thereby becoming more vulnerable to the surrendering process. And again, by "surrender," I don't mean giving up. To me, the act of surrender means to give yourself permission to live a centered life…from your soul's perspective; it means letting go of the control so that God can enter in and handle all of the details.

"True intelligence operates silently.
Stillness is where creativity and solutions to problems are found."
– Eckhart Tolle

So the question is, do you meditate? If not, have you thought about cracking on with it? If you choose to give it a shot, you will quickly realize its benefits. If you are not feeling the benefits, this usually means you haven't yet learned to quiet your mind. And don't fall prey to the whole "I can't sit still that long" excuse. Or to the "My mind is too busy" justification. These are limiting ways in which to approach this highly beneficial practice. So find a way to persevere, because it will not take long for you to feel meditation's undeniable value. For some it helps to simply stare into the distance in total observation; this is a wonderful method of slowing your mind prior to learning to meditate. There are many forms of meditation from which to choose (Zen, Tonglen, Transcendental, etc.). But the important part is to find the practice that works best for you. For those of you who have been meditating for years, maybe it's time to deepen your experience, or experiment with a new practice unknown to you. I've been consistently meditating for years now. I enjoy it immensely, and am fully open to the process of going deeper and learning more each day.

"Meditate. Live purely. Be quiet. Do your work with mastery.
Like the moon, come out from behind the clouds! Shine."
– Buddha

Here are some of the benefits I reap from my own meditation practice: First and foremost, meditation is a place where I can quiet my mind; a still mind will provide rest. Also, meditation takes me away from the utter chaos and noise that incessantly surrounds me— it provides me a certain effortlessness as I walk through life. If you want to hear God or have creativity come to you, you must go into silence. I mean, how can you hear a friend speaking if the television is blaring, the kids are screaming, or the dog is barking? So you turn off the television, give the kids a snack, and feed the dog. Now you have created a quiet environment in which to hear your friend speak.

In landscape design, the most successful gardens have areas of grass amongst vast plantings, so the eyes have a chance to rest, breathe, and appreciate. Get my drift?

> "You need not do anything. Remain sitting at your table
> and listen. You need not even listen, just wait. You need
> not even wait, just learn to be quiet, still, and solitary.
> And the world will freely offer itself to you unmasked.
> It has no choice, it will roll in ecstasy at your feet."
> – Franz Kafka

When you meditate, you are in the "space" between your thoughts…or you are in the "gap," as it's been said. This is where you receive answers to your questions, by opening your direct connection to God. Yes, the gap can be fleeting, lasting merely a couple of seconds—but as you become more proficient in your practice, your time in the gap will increase. You will eventually feel the lightness of being in bliss.

> "Be still. Stillness reveals the secrets of eternity."
> – Lao Tzu

When you first begin to meditate, this practice may not work for you. This can happen for a couple of reasons: either you don't quite understand what you are supposed to do, or the particular meditation practice you are undergoing is not right for you. Either way, I've been told there's no such thing as a "bad" meditation. As long as you are attempting to quiet your mind—in one form or another—you are on the right track. Many Buddhists suggest that meditation is simply the discipline of sitting with yourself for a few minutes each day—and it's not necessarily the "success" of the individual sitting that matters. If you are interested in learning how to meditate, I suggest Wayne

Dyer's, *Getting in the Gap*. This is a very simple book that explains meditation in practical terms, how it can help you, and how to do it. There is also a guided meditation disc included in the book.

> "Emancipate yourself from mental slavery;
> none but ourselves can free our minds."
> – Bob Marley

Here are some meditation tips:

Prepare for your meditation by releasing any negative thought patterns at least 30 minutes prior to beginning. Replace your "bad" thoughts with good-feeling vibrations and positive energy.

Do not take your stress and anxiety into your practice. You will not have a quality meditation if you rush into it or bring baggage with you.

Choose a comfortable place where you will be undisturbed. Sit in your favorite chair or go out into your yard. I like to drive to the lake near my home and park my car. I find it quite relaxing to recline the seat back, and simply enjoy my surroundings prior to getting started.

Then for five or 10 minutes, put all of your energy toward feeling happy. Start to slow your mind and "just be." Then simply observe your surroundings without thinking about them, or placing any judgment upon them. See the gull in flight, but don't think about it. Observe the joggers' stride, but give them no thought, either. Don't judge anything you see. Just observe. Now begin to notice your breath.

Smile and allow yourself to feel good. Breathe deeply several times, begin focusing inward, close your eyes, and meditate.

It is best to start your day with a 10- to 20-minute meditation. This sets a peaceful tone for your morning, as well as the rest of your day. A first-thing-in-the-morning meditation practice can offer you a delightful state of mind, allowing you to move elegantly forward with your day, hour by hour. If you can make the time, meditate again during the evening. As you become more accustomed to this practice, and its benefits, you will find yourself wanting to snatch mini meditations throughout your day. And yes, "zoning out" is actually a form of meditation, so take advantage of it!

"In the midst of movement and chaos, keep stillness inside of you."
– Dr. Deepak Chopra

Without question, the highlight of my day is the moment I come out of my meditation. This gives me an immense sense of peace; possibilities permeate my Being. Those of you who have been meditating for some time will know this feeling. Every now and then, you will find yourself very deeply in the gap. It is purity. It is all possibilities. You will find it.

"...when you meditate, you bring God's silent love into your
present moments. In silence and stillness God's energy will
become yours. By slowing your mind and other thoughts,
you allow the fastest vibrations of spirit to enter. That
faster vibration is one of harmony, love, and peace."
– Dr. Wayne Dyer

For me, meditation is the key to keeping to my spiritual Path. The difficulties you face will wither in the presence of a peaceful mind. Soon peacefulness through meditation will become the foundation of your spiritual life, and this will make everything I mention in this book a lot simpler to implement. Cultivating a peaceful, quieter mind has a way of softening the sharp edges of life. And it is this state of mind that provides me with a sense of peace, which allows joy to be at the forefront of my life.

Reading and Listening

Are you a reader? Funny question to ask while you are reading this book!

Since you are beginning this new metaphysical shift, you most likely have "the fever"—which means you are probably feeling like a sponge for all things spiritual. Am I correct? Well, to this day, I can't get my hands on enough spiritual content, and this continues to be a major source of inspiration for me. I learn so much from various mystical masters by reading their books and watching their videos. This being said, I suggest you grab anything you can get your hands on! If it feels good, give it a try! There are so many spiritual concepts on which you can focus: e.g., detachment, allowing, awareness, Nature, alignment, changing your thoughts, living in the moment, intention, non-judgment, meditation, etc.

Yes, the list is long and fascinating, but don't feel overwhelmed. Remember, everything is connected, so you will eventually come around to all of these concepts. In fact, you will operate with keen awareness fairly early on in your development. One or two of the concepts will probably resonate with you right from the beginning, making you hyper-focused on each one to follow, as you practice to truly understand them all.

Always keep in mind you are allowed to learn at your own pace. The key is to look for the clues and signs throughout your day that will bring you to your next teaching. For example, you may see something in an advertisement or a movie. Or you may go to a seminar where the presenter mentions how powerful a certain practice is—and the next thing you know you are implementing said practice into your day-to-day life. And the success of a new practice will give you the confidence you need to keep moving forward with new ideas. So just read and study as much as you can. Sooner or later, you will form your own spiritual Layer Cake—your unique practice—as other ideas and concepts begin to sing to you. (More on this soon...)

Just Keep to Your Path by applying what feels right, and your inimitable process will eventually develop on its own. Most spiritual students begin by emulating what other people are doing who are farther along on their Path. And if what they're doing works for you...excellent! If not, move in another direction. Remember, everything has its season. In fact, this book may not be right for you at this time...but in a month, or a year, or in 14 years, it may be just what you need!

Daily mantras

In my own experience along my Path, I have found it helpful to use mantras all day long; I think it's important to have one for every situation. You will come across many mantras throughout your spiritual research, and you can also create your own. Mantras act as saviors. When I need a mantra, I call this my "Swerve." In other words, I use my mantras to *Swerve* around the stress or anxiety associated with any particular issue.

The number one mantra I used when I first stepped onto my Path (and continue to use every day) is: *"Everything is as it should be."* When you grasp the value of this statement, you bring a new reality into your fold because you have put "selur" in neutral, and this can redirect you into a more peaceful state. This is your awareness in action! This is you looking *within* for solutions. This is you growing and developing spiritually.

When you practice awareness by using a mantra to shift out of a strenuous situation, you realize in that moment your life is in your own hands, and that you really do control your own destiny. To realize that your thoughts and feelings actually drive your life experience forward, is to know you are a Creator. You then begin taking responsibility for your own situation, and your innate conscious awareness starts to kick in on its own. That said, you know now your world is exactly as it should be because the Universe is in perfect balance. And herein rests the beauty of balance: You can change your reality by addressing how you feel about every aspect of your life!

Low on money? Don't have enough to pay the bills? Here comes the stress! I can see it coming from a mile away! So do you want to know what *my* Swerve is for this predicament? *"I am abundant in all areas of my life. Thank you, God, for every penny I have!"* Or, if I'm wondering how I'm going to make it after paying all my bills and having nothing left until payday, I Swerve by saying to myself, *"I'm so thankful all of my bills are paid!"* Then I switch to visions of financial abundance, and having plenty in the bank for everything I need and desire. And these kind of mantras, combined with accompanying visualizations, allow me to minimize my stress level or, better yet, keep the stress from impacting me on any level at all. Now I've established some sacred space, and am able to consider creative solutions, as opposed to just feeling pressured and lashing out. Cyclical thoughts be gone!

Feeling low or flat? Wondering where the joy is today? We all have a down moment or two on occasion. What to do? Well, since you are now "participating" in your life in lieu of "spectating" your way through it, how do you Swerve around feeling depressed for no apparent reason? Try this Swerve from one of our earlier exercises: Walk up to a mirror, take a few deep breaths, and with an open mind say out loud: *"I Love myself."* Say this at least 20 times and allow a smile to come across your face. You may be smiling because you feel silly, hoping nobody discovers you during this practice of merriment! But whatever the case, this will lead to a better state of mind, putting you in a great mood!

Remember, you are not your labels or your conditioned coatings, so allow the tumult coursing through your system to melt away. The more you practice your mantras, the sooner non-judgment—toward yourself and others—becomes second nature. And before you know it, you are living a more joyful life because you don't allow external conditions to impede your progress anymore. Keep to Your Spiritual Path by loving yourself and *feeling* internally that you are worthy of giving and receiving Love.

Beginning your day? After you have said your "thank yous" and have set your intentions for the day, say to yourself, *"It's going to be a great day!"* and really *feel* it! What a great mantra with which to start your morning! Just set the expectation that something awesome will happen in your day! Give yourself the opportunity to believe in the magic of this day's possibilities…that you *know* something good is coming your way! It's not important to know what it is; once again, let the Universe take care of those details. But stay aware and present, because that special something can come your way at any moment. And when it happens, you will appreciate it and be mesmerized by how the Law of Attraction works so flawlessly (and how reliable it is!).

The morning is the best time to keep your mantras flowing, because the day is young, which means so much more can still manifest at that point. Armed with this feeling of limitless potential, go forth into your day with your chin held high, expecting wonderful miracles to flow through you all day. Look for an opportunity to give while you are receiving something awesome. Set yourself up to receive the goodness and to pass it on to everyone with whom you come in contact. You get the idea!

The following is a list of "Swerve mantras," which have always worked very well for me. So apply the ones that resonate with you, or try creating your own!

Everything is as it should be
Non-judgment today
Give something special today
I love myself
Thank you for...
...the abundance that surrounds me
...my excellent health
...all of the money I have
...my family
...my work
I create my reality
I am abundant
Stay in the moment
God is within me
It's gonna be a great day
I love you
I feel light
I feel positive
Minimize
Something good is about to happen
There is no Path to happiness...happiness is the Path
The joy of liberation
I attract that which I am

I create my reality
Stay plugged in
I am...
...loving
...healthy
...wealthy
...honest
...peaceful
Just be
Participate
Manifest in freedom
Live with joy
Love

Triggers and Events

The following is a unique method I developed in the beginning of my journey, because I knew I had the potential at that time to deviate from my Path. So, using my smartphone, I set "mantra events" to alert and remind me of how I wanted to feel throughout a particular day. This was especially important in the beginning, as I was trying to eliminate judgment, learning to become aware through participation, while continually reminding myself of how abundant our world really is.

The point I want to make here is that these "mantra events" always seemed to come just when I needed them the most. Just as a challenge would arise, when it was easier and more comfortable for me to "spectate" instead of "participate," my phone would send me an enlightened event: *"Thank you for my excellent health!"* And then I would feel the relief, which helped me to create a new chain of thoughts, and this made me smile. So in my spiritual infancy, programming my phone in this manner helped me to Swerve, so I could better remain in the present moment, and move forward while doing so. These mantra events—that I continue to program into my phone to this day—have become a symbol of abundance for me.

I typically have eight to 10 mantra events programmed in my phone at any given time, which I use every day. They are always evolving depending on the new lessons I'm learning or beginning to apply. Or maybe I'm struggling in a particular area and need the additional help. Well, all of the "Swerve mantras" I previously listed have, at some point, been an event on my phone. Long story short, give this technique a shot, because this may prove to be an invaluable tool for you, too! But remember to give respect to your events. When they sound, regardless of how busy you may be, give a few seconds of attention to: *"I create my own reality!"* Or: *"I love myself and I'm doing a great job!"*

You can even use these phone events as a reminder to send a greeting card to someone, or to do something nice for yourself. But again, don't dismiss your events…otherwise they have no value. When you ignore them, you are ignoring an opportunity to Love and invest in yourself. Sure, you may drive a few people mad because your phone sounds throughout the day, but you will all be better off because of it! So which events have you already set for yourself today?

Do what makes you joyful

Looking for another starting point along your Path? Well then, do things that make you feel good! Yup, it's as simple as that! Okay, enough said…onto the next tool! Seriously, think about the impact you can have on your psyche if you're doing something that fulfills you. For example, I'm one of those strange folks who loves to pull weeds in the garden. I know, I know…but for some reason, I find this task very relaxing. And I never wear gloves, so my hands take quite the beating. It's worth it to me, though, because this allows me to feel connected to the Earth—yes, I find weeding to be a joyful activity that opens my mind to the miracles and balance of Nature.

So the question is, what are the hobbies or interests that instantly put *you* into a groovy state of mind? Now imagine a life full of such activities. I mean, that's part of your dream, right? To do what you Love, and to live from that state of joy? So the next question is, does your ideal life grant you the time to practice your favorite interests? Or does it offer you the space to finally learn how to hang glide or scuba dive? Get out that dusty bowling ball in the red vinyl bag that has been hibernating underneath the stairs for nine years—that is, if bowling is something you Love to do. Or what about those paint brushes tucked away in the back closet that you never use? When was the last time they touched a canvas? Or perhaps brewing your own beer was once an enjoyable hobby for you? I have a friend who used to build kites; he misses it tremendously. Are you getting my point, here?

As spiritual and human Beings, we are meant to use our minds, and to move our bodies—we were all born to be creative! So stop merely "going through the motions" of life, day after day after day. Find your dance. Do things you know will "float your boat." If these things keep you carefree and creative, then why not? The act of being creative with *anything*—even tonight's dinner!—will put you in a better mood. And why not encourage your family and friends to do the same? Put down that remote control. Stop wasting your life in front of the TV, only to find out what's going on in *other* people's lives. I mean, it's one thing to relax by watching a little TV for an hour or so—but imagine how much of your life you've missed due to staring at it for five or six hours every night, for decades on end!? Once again, it's your choice. Oh, and consider what might happen if you choose to stop digesting hour after hour of those depressing news broadcasts? Yes, be informed, but do so with moderation and common sense. You think reality TV is entertaining? Well, from where I sit, it really does nothing more than promote imbalanced drama and unhealthy competition (something "selur" totally gets off on), so keep *that* in mind!

I challenge you to turn off your TV for one month. That's right— give yourself 30 days to see what you can do with your life with absolutely no distractive television of any kind. Until you begin experimenting with these kind of alternate lifestyle choices, you will have no idea how much you can accomplish, and how much your need for TV (and/or negative media) decreases your ability to heal yourself and move forward with your dreams. Letting go of media addictions is yet another form of freedom that can be attained along the spiritual Path. Occasional sporting events and movies aside, your life will expand in all areas when you unplug the TV, and tune into your creative Source!

Once the TV is safely turned off (with the remote securely locked away!), pick up the book you've been wanting to read, or go for a stroll through your neighborhood. Reengage yourself with society face-to-face and feel your life-force increase for the better. Start becoming accountable for the promises you've made to yourself. If you say, "I will begin right now," then do so and stick with it! This will lead to a cleaner-feeling life. Following through on the things you promise yourself is a profound form of self-love, and will escort you to greater accomplishments! I have recently placed a higher degree of focus on doing the things I want/could/should do...and the result has been liberating! I had no idea how much putting these things off was impacting my subconscious mind, and I now feel much less pressure in my life because of it. I feel as though that thin layer in my mind has somehow been cleansed, opening up a new feeling of, "What's next?" for me. Unreal...

Visualization

I use the power of visualization every day in my life; I use my mind's eye to see pictures of my desires in order to *feel* what it is I want. Because when I can *feel* it, it usually manifests itself through the Law of Attraction, or helps me to feel a greater sense of joy. And I know, through infinite patience, that my felt desires are on their way. I also know that limiting beliefs will keep my desires from arriving, so I don't give much energy to negative thoughts anymore. What I mean is, my visualizations includes *only* my desires...end of story. I visualize traveling to exotic destinations, positive outcomes to the circumstances of my days, how I want to live and how I want to feel, and so on.

The idea of manifesting desires is a very mysterious thing. There are many facets of the human thought process that have to be in sync, in order for you to consciously bring the people, situations, and things into your physical life that you truly do desire. Many teachers have compared the Law of Attraction to other universal laws (such as the Law of Gravity, for instance), in an effort to explain how manifesting really works. For example, when you drop a rock from a ladder, you have the expectation the rock will hit the ground, right? Because, through the Law of Gravity, of course it will hit the ground! And we've been raised not to dispute this law in any way.

Well, the Law of Attraction works exactly the same way. But we have been taught from the beginning of time how *not* to leverage it. The problem is, most people request things from God, or from the Universe, while situated in a cognitive position of lack. "Please, Universe," they plead, "I'm so broke. Please let my check be bigger this month. Please let me get that raise." But what they are really doing in this moment is telling the Universe and/or God how broke they are, thereby attracting more "broke-ness" into their lives. But if they were to ask for things from a cognitive state of *abundance*, they then set the stage for that manifestation to light up their world! Remember, like attracts like…so let's try this instead: "Thank you, Universe, for my upcoming paycheck, which is enough to pays all of my bills. And since the raise I desire has already been approved, I'm asking and expecting my paycheck to be 20 percent higher this month."

The Universe is abundantly rich and, therefore, you have the right to ask for what is yours. In other words, ask for exactly what you want, humbly and gratefully, and don't forget to implement a specific timeline of when you would like your wish to arrive.

Your belief in the arrival of your desire needs to be just as committed and solid as your belief that the rock dropped from the ladder will, indeed, hit the ground.

Anything less and your desire will stay in the Universe's holding pattern. Learn to stoke your inherent ability to manifest and flood yourself with your desires.

Most people know that winning athletes practice visualizing a successful performance prior to a competition. It's true, the practice of visualization has begun to permeate into mainstream society, as a technique for helping people realize their dreams. But for our context here, we are going to use visualization to generate an emotional response, because it's the emotional response which leads to a chain of positive thoughts. Those thoughts will then lead to the feeling of having attained your desire. Since we live an energetic existence, your positive signals sent to the Universe will bounce back to you in the form of great things. As long as you have no limiting thoughts, your desires will arrive through the Law of Attraction.

Now here's the thing: Some of you will be able to take this practice and manifest your dreams very quickly. For you, it is easier to focus on positive things, while eliminating the poison from your mind. For other people, however, it will take longer. But it's in this realization that you are experiencing the Law in full force. The Law is telling you that your outdated, cyclical ways of thinking are responsible for keeping your desires at bay. This is the Law in action. So just keep washing the stain from the rag. Change your thoughts and feel the flow of good things. If you want to test manifestation, start with a small "ask." From there, you will know what to do.

I believe holding a particular vision in my mind for at least 90 seconds allows me to fully develop the feeling of obtaining my desire. Of course, there are various manifestation techniques you can use. You can either visualize in your mind having already received your desire, allowing the great feelings to flood through you as if the desire has already come to pass. Or, you can imagine having a conversation during which your desire is actually taking place. I tend to use the latter a bit more.

Here's how I like to visualize:

Once the desire enters my mind, I run through the internal dialogue or "conversation" surrounding said desire. As the conversation develops, I allow myself to begin truly feeling what I will experience when it actually does happen.

As I am writing this book, I have a strong desire to go to the Caribbean. Let us say I want to fly to Barbados for some relaxation, but I need life to fall into place for the trip to manifest. Therefore, my visualization goes something like this:

My phone rings: *"Hey Spencer. It's Roy. Just wanted to let you know your book was picked up by a major publishing house! And they're giving you a nice advance on your next book, plus you have 18 months to complete it!"* (Now, in my mind, I imagine myself listening to the words and allowing myself to feel *real* excitement, as if this were an actual conversation.)

"Wow, Roy! That's incredible! Thank you so much for calling! I have some great ideas I need to sort out in order to get going with my next writing project. So I need to get away from the chaos for a while to get my ideas in order." (Now I'm feeling the rush of booking the plane tickets. I'm picturing myself playing in the sand, swimming, and yes, putting my thoughts together for the next book.)

"I totally get it, Spence. Do whatever you have to do. What do you have in mind?"

"Well, we've always wanted to go back to the tropics, so this gives us the headspace and finances to pull it off. I'm so excited! This is a dream come true! Thanks again for all of your hard work on this, Roy; I appreciate it a great deal!" (The joy running through my system is intense by now; I make no apologies for the awesomeness I'm feeling in this moment!)

"You're welcome. I know it's your life's work to help people as best you can. And this trip will give you another avenue to do just that." (When I've finished the conversation, I wallow in utter joy for 10 to 15 seconds, because I know this trip will actually manifest for me.)

I know visualization works; it's just up to me to keep my limiting thoughts at a distance, and to simply believe the Universe will provide. Develop your own ability to visualize, and hold your ultimate visions in your mind for at least a minute or two. While envisioning, do not let any thoughts outside of your desire creep in. This is your time and it belongs to you! The absolute key is to *feel* the emotions associated with your particular desire. For any specific desire, visualize it at least three times each day. Just like with anything else, you will become more proficient with this over time.

Soon, the practice of visualization will become an irreplaceable tool in your spiritual garden shed!

STEPPING STONE: This is the point where I want you to go beyond just writing down your dream life. It's time now for you to start a second list of "action items" you'll need to take in order to make your move. That's right, I want you to actually begin formulating the steps you need to take to realize your dream. The more you plan for it, the more it becomes a part of you. *Expect* your desires to arrive. Through infinite patience, eliminating limiting beliefs, and walking a Path of recognized abundance, you will, indeed, realize all of your desires. It's happening to me right now! I opened my mind to my dharma, and now I'm sitting here writing a book, which can support you in your own efforts to Keep to Your Spiritual Path. I mean, how cool is *that*? Allow this philosophy to flow and grow, and this will happen for you as well!

And now for one more tip on visualization: From Deepak Chopra, I learned to go over my dream list at night, just prior to going to sleep. So first, I run through the awesomeness of my day, focusing on the top five things I experienced that I am truly grateful for. Then I read and recite to myself my imagined dream life. This process helps to reprogram the subconscious at a deeper level, while also providing the basis wonderful night's sleep! And after this practice I always awake feeling full of gratitude the next morning. It's gonna be another great day!

The little things matter

It's time to step up the details in your world to improve your overall Quality of Life. This is huge. I mean, why do people use their best china only when guests are over for Thanksgiving? And why do they short-change themselves by using the chipped, secondary dishes the rest of the year? Put the kibosh on that right now! Improve your everyday Quality of Life by using the good stuff...all the time! Put a flower in a vase. Take a moment to breathe in and appreciate the sweet air when you step outside. Read a book before bedtime instead of watching TV. (In fact, if you have a TV in the bedroom, remove it! Falling asleep with the news, reality TV, violence or any form of drama is counter-productive to your spiritual growth). Plant a tree. Bake some bread. Love up your pet. Take a stroll through the market and let your senses run wild! Learn to slow down your hurried pace and your overtaxed mind. Start to reevaluate and question how you can improve *everything* in your life. You owe it to yourself!

Sit, stay, and enjoy your coffee or tea, instead of grabbing it to go, while racing off to your next stop. Better yet, instead of going to the usual corporate coffee chain, start supporting a smaller, more sophisticated, independently owned café. Treat yourself!

Being good to yourself through the minute details is another area in which your self-awareness can help you. Once you start upgrading everything in your life, your self-worth begins to improve. And by "upgrade," I don't necessarily mean spending a bunch of money you may not have in order to get the best of everything. In fact, I recommend focusing more on the little nuances, such as:

- Instead of saying a mere, "Hello?" when your phone rings, say, "This is Eva!"
- Instead of drinking out of can, pour your beverage into a glass.
- Instead of fast-food, support family-owned sandwich shop that sources organically.
- Instead of just mowing and pulling the weeds, plant a small veggie patch.
- Instead of taking the faster, but more congested route home, take the scenic country road.
- Instead of buying new shoes, give your old shoes new life with a nice polish.
- Instead of eating in front of the TV, enjoy a meal with your family at the dinner table.
- Instead of living with a dirty windshield, take nine minutes to clean it, inside and out.
- Instead of slouching in your chair, sit up straight and exhibit pride in your good posture.

- Instead of driving 200 feet to your next stop, enjoy the fresh air and take the short walk.
- Instead of walking with your nose down, lift your chin and appreciate the sky.
- Instead of the same 'ol thing, be spontaneous and do something different.
- Instead of saying "someday," why not do it *today*?

So you see, elevating the little things in your life will lead you to feeling better. You get the idea. So go do some little things for yourself, and for those around you.

STEPPING STONE: If peace in your life is something you treasure, it is important you seek quiet moments. They are easily attainable, because the opportunity surrounds you all day. Decluttering your mind and giving it the chance to rest, even momentarily, can have a huge impact on your wellbeing.

Would you like to instantly increase your Quality of Life? Then. Put. Your. Devices. Down! You don't need to look at your phone *all* day. Do you know most people check their smartphones a staggering 221 times per *day*? If you are awake for 18 hours, that comes to 12 times every hour, or about every five minutes! Are you serious, people? I mean, *really!* And if you are not using your phone, do you have to have it right next to you at all times "just in case"? Your phone is a tool, not an oxygen tank. And it doesn't have the answers you seek…you do! So why feel so compelled to retort immediately to every ringtone or notification? Why be a slave to your phone and allow it to run your life? Besides, this is the antithesis of the "participating" theory I've been talking about…remember?

I *believe* you can have a much more peaceful life if you were to minimize your phone usage. On that note, I'd like to issue you a challenge to cut your phone use in half. Whatever this may mean to you, find a way to text, post, call, email, surf, or check your phone 50 percent less than you do today. This may seem like a monumental task but, when you really think about it, it should not be so difficult.

(By the way, I'm very curious to hear about the results this stepping stone has in your life, so be sure to let me know the impact it has made.)

If you have high-anxiety even *thinking* about phone separation, consider starting small. Because each time you unplug, you create the potential for a moment of peace and, therefore, growth. You can start small by leaving your phone in the car when you grocery shop or fill your tank. And don't bring it with you when you go for a run. Leave it in your bedroom while you are having dinner or relaxing. Do you remember how we all got along just fine prior to "smart" phones?

Devices have conditioned the minds of many people to live in short bursts, and to be always and perpetually "available." The thought of sustained "Beingness" has become totally foreign to those now addicted to our technological world. That's why it's so important to participate in your life and harken for a less chaotic mind by taking scheduled media breaks from time to time. String together sustained moments of peace by occasionally putting aside your distracting devices. Go sit at the coffee shop and just enjoy yourself. Just be in the now. Relax. Maybe even read a *real* book... you know, the kind with paper pages and a cover? Step up the little things in your life, and watch the quality of it improve for the better. Give yourself a chance...

Here is another great concept:

Write down some ideas that may help someone other than yourself. In James Altucher's *Choose Yourself,* he talks about how we can all cure our brain's atrophy by brainstorming 10 unique ideas per day. That is 3,650 ideas per year—wow! Can you imagine what you can create from this process?

Another thing you can do to improve your Quality of Life is to rearrange, reorganize, and clean out your home/garage/office. Simplify your life and feel space open up in your mind! Deep-clean your home. Put on some rubber gloves and scour out the corners. Hang a favorite photo or a print of a beautiful mountain in the garage or in some other random place within your home. Use this decluttering process as a symbol of your new life. Recondition your place, while simultaneously reconditioning your mind...it all goes hand-in-hand. Through this process, you will feel refreshed, making it easier to tackle other aspects of your life.

Take an inventory of your life. Look at the areas where you have been "cutting corners" or maybe have been a little lazy. Remember, you want to upgrade your life so you can stand up for your wellbeing! So try taking a bit more care by allowing yourself to elevate the micro-components of your existence. Improve your posture by sitting up straight. Use the nicer stationary when you write to a friend. Be thoughtful as you shop for a present (instead of buying yet another gift-card from the grocery store endcap). Be *that* person. Tell someone, "I love you," just because…

Elevating the small things in life may not sound like much, but I promise you the sum of your efforts will seriously pay off. You will feel lighter, less encumbered; you will become nimble and be able to adjust on the fly!

Greetings and salutations

I'm of German heritage, and I've been very fortunate to have spent a huge portion of my life in this part of the world. In Germany, a formal handshake is mandatory with everyone with whom you come in contact. This is a customary practice, showing that you respect and honor the person with whom you are interacting. A friend of my family, named Wolf, has turned his greetings and salutations into an art form. And it's no coincidence Wolf is The Cyclone's (Onkel Jakob's) son. When he greets you, his handshake is firm, but warm. He looks directly and gently into your eyes, and from heart will tell you how happy he is to see/meet you. His greetings last a little longer than you are accustomed to, and sometimes it feels like he's lingering a bit. But it feels okay, because you recognize you are in the presence of someone extraordinary. You feel special when interacting with Wolf, and immediately want to begin honoring this German tradition in your own unique way.

Wolf is also a natural conversationalist. He truly listens to people and is interested in their lives. He offers intelligent insight and humor, albeit he is a bit of a gossiper. But he truly is a joy. After having a meal or spending some time with him, you inevitably wonder what the goodbye experience will be like. Then, when it finally happens, you are so stunned by how much he genuinely expresses his appreciation of your company, you glaze over a bit thinking, *Who is this person? Who does this?* His is an honorable custom, which I submit should be reintroduced to all of mankind. I am always trying to improve myself in this area, because taking a genuine interest in other people shows sincere compassion. So become a master of the greeting, the goodbye, and of the spoken and written salutation as well. Become reengaged with humanity. Take the time to make everyone you meet feel special. Become *that* person.

Reengage

Reengage with your fellow man! Make it a point to be someone's daylight today. Shine onto everyone you touch. Regardless of how shy you may be, or how disappointed you are in your fellow citizens, just learn to open yourself up to them again. Who have you become today? Well, whatever happened to you in your life, don't blame it on other people. You make your own choices regarding how you are going to feel, remember? There was a time in your life when you did engage—remember, you were eight years old! You said, "Hi!" to everyone with no fear. You made friends everywhere you went. Bravo if you still do this. If not, just begin doing it again and reap the benefits!

Release an honest smile to someone and observe what happens. If you are learning a new language in a foreign town, a great way to reengage is to try your new Italian vocabulary on a shop owner who will understand you. When you say, "How are you?" do it with conviction and a caring demeanor, as if you really want to hear the response. Engaging with people will help you open your mind to your purpose. After all, we're all here to help each other. Walking your Path with a fearless mindset will open you to so many otherwise unseen and unrealized opportunities. So stop letting them pass you by...be the person you want to be.

If you haven't already figured it out, we're all connected. Treating people only as beloved family members will help you realize our unity. Look forward to every type of human, animal, and environmental interaction you will have on this beautiful day. Maintain eye contact and your smile a split-second longer, all the while appreciating the serendipitous response you receive in return. You just made a positive impact on someone's life—*yes!* Then walk away feeling fantastic and overjoyed for having experienced that opportunity! Embrace the shared bond you have with other living things with gusto! When you do this, your life will thrive! This type of changed perspective roots you deeper into your Path of goodness and joy.

Our current time on this earth is borrowed from our children. We are here to be stewards of this beautiful Earth for the coming generations. Harmony is our opportunity, so don't squander it... live it! And don't just take from it, give back to the Earth in any way you can.

I hope you have garnered a lot of good ideas so far. But tell me, are certain tools or techniques resonating with you more than others? This typically is the case because we're all unique in our own way and, therefore, your practice will take on its own flavor, in its own time. The next section is all about finding your individual way along your Path, while opening your eyes to how you can let your practice fall into place by itself. What flavor is your cake?

PART III
Totality

A new dawn has arrived. Inspired by the pure unity of all living things, a loving, creative life has sparked and gelled, allowing your purpose to sing and generosity to thrive.

BELIEF NINE
Your Spiritual Layer Cake

The Yukon Cornelius effect.

To help you Keep to Your Spiritual Path, I've presented several ideas throughout the course of this book, such as:

- *Why?* you want to walk a spiritual Path
- *Defining* your Path, by knowing how it should look and feel for you
- *How* to travel along your unique and individual Path
- *Keeping* to it, by implementing a new belief system that provides you with the tools to do so

Now we'll dig a little deeper by taking a look at what your future may hold in the coming months and years.

Over time, you will be implementing many of the techniques outlined within this book, along with other teachings you will pick up along the way. With your new heightened awareness in place, my hope is that you will now be feeling much better about the direction of your life. It may seem as though you have a long journey ahead, but your "edginess"(your defeating attitude which was so pervasive only a few weeks ago) should now be greatly minimized. And that self-defeating emotional state has hopefully been replaced with better, higher, and more joyful feelings. For in reducing angst and frustration, only joy and sunshine can prevail. And it is this higher-vibrational state that can provide a compounding effect, vaulting you toward committing to this new belief system at a much deeper level. My sincere wish, therefore, is that you are thrilled with your progress thus far. Maybe you are feeling the positive effects of your new meditation practice? Or perhaps you have experienced the thrill of extending unconditional generosity to your fellowman? Whatever the case, I'm sure it is beginning to come together for you now.

So you are evolving down your Path. Now what?

Once you begin feeling and reaping the instant benefits of the spiritually natured beliefs presented in this book, your thirst for more information will probably begin to explode. You will look forward each morning to the potential of your day, and you'll do so with a curious mind. You will be feeling much better and will see more contrast in your life and in the world around you. Yes, your heightened awareness will also open your eyes to the negativity and dysfunction in the world—but this is okay, because the dark and the light work together, providing a contrast by which you can better form your desires. In other words, knowing what you *don't* want helps to define what you *do* want.

Remember, it is important to wake each morning with the curiosity of the coming day's excellence and the lessons you will learn. Through each issue you face, remain positive, aware, and present without fail. Just Keep to Your Spiritual Path day by day, and you'll continue to progress. Remember, developing a foundational practice for yourself means it will be there for you when you need it the most!

Your flexibility and thirst for knowledge serves as an indicator that you are open to many ideas now. If you are a person whom is truly committed to Keeping to Your Spiritual Path, you will begin reading, watching, and listening to all things spiritual. If you keep a journal, begin writing whatever comes to mind. Maybe you'll have questions regarding awakenings. Or perhaps you'll feel compelled to jot down a phrase your friend said during a particular conversation. Journaling can be a great way to start an inventory of your new thoughts and ideas because, in writing them down, you're making a conscious effort to mentally sort through them. When you read back over the entries in your journal, you can then teach yourself how to best weave together your new perceptions, epiphanies, and beliefs. But the important part is to remain open to new information, which will continue to propel your growth. Note the spiritual language you pick up on from movies and in surrounding conversations. Take note of the philosophies that deeply resonate with you. And before long, you will begin drawing like-minded people into your experience. And then you may start to wonder when your dharma is going to present itself. Life will become exciting! And it's at this time when you will organically begin your "spiritual cross-training."

Mixing it up:

Now it's time to learn how to set intentions regarding your own spiritual Path, and what you want to create *along* that Path. The moment is *now* that you begin in earnest your commitment to personal growth. As you've been reading this book, you may have already begun implementing the *Fresh Beliefs* approach. Or maybe not. Either way, you may still be wayward, as you search for the right starting point. So let's do that now by taking a stance against the ego:

Through a simple, yet powerful declaration, you can determine the flow of your life: "From this point forward, I declare ownership of my thoughts and feelings. I declare my heightened awareness to be my top priority, and will leverage it to remain laser-focused on positive thought patterns at all times."

A declaration such as this puts a stamp on your life, making an immediate impact. It is your own willful revolution to detach from the ego, by emphatically claiming your independence from it. Return to yourself *now* what has been held captive from you for so many years. Free yourself and feel the fresh air of liberation, as you plant your *Fresh Beliefs* flag deep into the soil. Your declaration represents your freedom, so anchor yourself to what is rightfully yours: peace and love. Declare it *now!*

With your declaration established and in place, be prepared to use your commitment immediately, because "selur" will probably challenge you right away. If you deviate from your Path, it is usually because "selur" has reared its ugly head, or because you have simply plateaued during your practice. But this can cease in happening if you continually inject yourself with new ideas, concepts, and exercises, which represent your daily practice. And the origin of these ideas comes from the fertile ground of...the world! For example, you may hear a promising athlete's interview, in which she speaks of an uncompromising view of her dreams. Or you may hear a lyric from an old song you never noticed before, which today has a new meaning for you. Or someone you have attracted into your life will suggest a book for your reading pleasure, and that material happens to be just what you need to take your next step forward. Better yet, someday you may be on a walk, or out running a few errands, when you hear a whisper—a hint of a thought quickly revealing to you a profound truth! I mean, how can you possibly become spiritually bored if you are being positively challenged every moment of your life? Perspective!

"Spiritual cross-training" is all about learning and applying multiple spiritual practices simultaneously...to lift your wellbeing, while determining what works best for you along your own Path. Your current emotional, mental, physical, and spiritual states are yours' alone. You have arrived "here" through your own conditioned patterns and learned behaviors. So in order to recondition your cognitive and emotional reflexes, you have to discover what works the best for you. Be like Yukon Cornelius and launch your pickaxe high in the sky! If it sticks in the ice, give it a lickety-split taste to see if you have struck silver or gold. In other words, if it feels right, do it. Wahooooooo!!!

If you are feeling unsure about a new spiritual concept to which you have been newly introduced, experiment with it a little longer to be certain this tool is in alignment with your particular stage of growth. Or perhaps try viewing the concept from a different perspective, to see if it can support you in a manner you have not yet considered. In the end, if it's just not for you, regardless of its popularity, then put it aside for now. It is not going anywhere, so you can address it when the time is right. This "figuring out" process can allow you to have a little more flexibility with the various teachings and techniques that come your way. The important part is to grasp and absorb into your Being those practices which resonate most profoundly with you; only you can determine what works best. Remember, you are your own best teacher.

With your increased enthusiasm, you may feel the urge to spring some spiritual knowledge or teachings upon those around you. This is a great thought, because you should always seek to elevate those who are a part of your life. Just keep in mind that some folks aren't yet ready for your good intentions, while others can be introduced to spirituality simply by feeling the power of your presence in the room. Sure, it may be very apparent to *you* that "the Path" is what we should all strive to journey upon, but everyone has their own season, just as you do. Long story short, it is best not to force your own beliefs and spiritual concepts upon anyone else.

Spiritual cross-training can be ever-evolving. I tend to read three or four books at a time, always having some kind of spiritual content present in my life. My point being, this volume of reading provides me with all sorts of ideas on how to become a better "living" person. It also assists me in developing new concepts to help others keep to their own Paths. And the same holds true for you. Through your awareness and/or openness to an abundance of spiritual content, you will be continually introducing new ideas and techniques into your routine. Maybe you will deepen your meditation practice through a book you read, or go on a spiritual retreat because of an enlightening DVD you watched. Or perhaps you decide that attending a yoga class may be just what you need, due to a suggestion made by your spiritual coach or counselor. And as you begin to determine what works best for you, based on the tutorial content that filters into your experience, your own spiritual Layer Cake will then start to form.

You see, the layers of your cake are the distilled spiritual elements that work best for you. And your soul is the awakened buttercream filling, holding it all together. And as your conscious awareness helps you to dissolve away past conditioning, your Quality of Life will inevitably improve, allowing you to live a more connected, effervescent existence, while ultimately lifting those around you.

Advantages of spiritual cross-training include:

- immediate results
- shortened learning curve
- increased awareness
- attracting more like-minded people
- maintaining a fun and interesting practice
- deeper levels of openness and flexibility
- improved ability to guide others down their respective Paths
- the exposing of other wonderful concepts and techniques

Ultimately, as you Keep to Your Spiritual Path, you will reach a place where life begins to just "click." At this time, it may seem and feel more natural to stay at your current spiritual and cognitive level—but don't stagnate! Keeping a forward momentum is especially important for you now, otherwise you may slide back a little bit. So when you come across a concept that fascinates you, but you aren't quite sure what it means or how to apply it, take your time in learning how that particular concept may be related to another. In other words, we can sometimes discover something new and unexpected about a particular philosophy, by better understanding the various topics related to it. And this can help us to continually move forward along our Path, and with our practice.

Also, if there is a "far out" concept of interest to you, don't jump into it if you are not yet ready. Allow your understanding of spiritual ideas to flow to you as they should; you can't rush it. Things like this will come to you naturally, in their own time.

Stepping stone: I'm now offering you one final exercise: If you were able to come back to this world after your spirit is finished in your body, as what—or who—would you return? And as such, how would you give back to all living things while living your new physical existence? Okay, I will go first: After much deliberation, I would like to come back to this world as a Western Red Cedar tree thriving deep in the Cascade mountain range. I would give back to all living things by using my girth, as well as my ability to generate oxygen for our planet. I would not take pride in my beauty or grandeur, but in my allowance of shared space amongst my fellow trees, as I provided a home to the forest's living things. I would bask in the knowing that, should I someday fall in a mighty storm, I would continue to give back by decomposing and fertilizing the Earth.

So what say you?

It's exciting to note there are deeper levels of consciousness and spiritual planes yet to be discovered by you and me. These truths go much deeper than what I'm offering here. There are magnificent mainstream spiritual teachers, and many other "under the radar" luminaries, providing great insight and experience; and you will learn much from all of them. You will attract the masters and their teachings as you need them, and when you are ready for them. Ultimately, though, it is *you* who is your greatest teacher. And if through applying the concepts in this book you are able to arrive at a deeper understanding of how the Universe works, then we will have accomplished something wonderful together. One by one we will all awaken.

Over time, you will take on a new way of feeling and thinking as you journey farther and farther along your Path. Your mind will expand in many different directions as you seek to know yourself at deeper and more profound levels. But there is an order to this expansion, that happens differently for everyone. Moving through different levels of spiritual experience really is a graduation of sorts, as your practice continues to mature and gel.

You will have many more epiphanies as your mind becomes ever more open and flexible. You will feel the old ways of thinking melt away with each new moment of clarity you experience. You will soon realize that your detachment from negative thought patterns has opened up your mind to allow for the state of enlightenment.

And one day you may very well be struck by something profound. For instance, you suddenly realize you haven't had a bad day for months. Nor can you recall the last time you were deeply upset or frustrated. Your ability to handle difficult situations has given you a much higher Quality of Life. There is a peace about your Being that brings a fresh spring to your step. You have discovered how to easily manifest your dreams. Your life is taking on the shape you have envisioned. You put your wellbeing ahead of all things, but are always in search of opportunities to be lovingly generous with whatever is required.

And now for the Root...

I call the convergence of "Love," "Awareness," and "Flexibility" (L.A.F.) "the Root." When you reach the moment your commitment to your spiritual practice converts permanently into exhilaration and "Beingness," you have successfully "rooted" yourself into your spiritual Path. And as a "rooted person," you find yourself well on your way to the growth for which you strive. You realize you are a spiritual Being, seeking opportunities to spread your peace and love. With each passing day, you come to experience that epiphanies are more commonplace, as you dial into the infinite potential you hold.

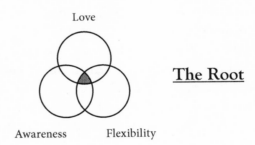

The Root

With the knowledge that *Love* is the core of your "Beingness," you live from the perspective of projecting your inner joy. And while in search of a deeper dimension of Love, you walk your Path with heightened *Awareness*, constantly checking in with yourself and evaluating how you feel in any given situation. Using your open mind to remain *Flexible*, you guide your emotions to a sunny place, giving turbulence no chance to invade your thoughts. These three principles put you in position to co-create a more positive, Love-filled life with

God. And the compounding effect *the Root* has on your *L.A.F.* will perpetually heighten, taking you ever closer to God-realization.

That said, I think it's about time I share with you *my* current practice. Coming up is not just what I do, but how I live. I've been implementing this practice for years now, and I can honestly tell you I love my life! Have I reached every goal? No, but I know I will. Do I radiate joy every moment of my existence? No, but I very rarely have a bad day. Do I still judge and/or have limiting thoughts? Of course! But far less than before I began my practice and, as such, I am in a great place emotionally because of what you are about to read.

BELIEF TEN
My Daily Practice

This is how I do it.

There is great joy in operating with genuine belief in how I live my moments. My daily practice, therefore, involves more than just "doing spiritual things." I view my practice as doing my part in my relationship with God. And since I am co-creating my life with God, I know God is responsible for bringing all things abundant to the table. So in order that I may do *my* part, I, too, must bring an abundant attitude to the table—I must align myself with all the gifts God has to offer. After all, I can't expect God to provide whatever it is I want along my mountainous journey, if I'm merely lollygagging down the base paths! So I give everything I have to my Creator, in each moment, as best I can, because I want to realize much in my life.

The day I gained true belief in the understanding that God and I are in this together was the day my life changed forever. Pam Grout writes in E2 that Jesus uses an Aramaic word when making a request of God. This word combines the ideas of "asking and demanding" into the distinct concept of requesting and receiving our God-given right to abundance. In other words, God will give me all that I ask/demand because God knows I am simply claiming my given right to unlimited abundance. For you to feel the same regarding *your* new belief system, leverage your vulnerability a bit, and allow the Ten Beliefs process to blossom as it will.

In the beginning, when I first stepped foot on the spiritual Path,

I spent a few months absorbing as much content as I could (books, conscious magazines, enlightening DVDs, seminars, etc.). And it was during this time that certain themes began to repeat themselves to me. So I listened intently and openly to many teachers and mentors who were all unique in their delivery and points of view. I began to recognize, though, that everything I was learning and beginning to apply to my life comes from the seed of what I call "Spiritual Love." Now yes, we all have felt Love at one time or another in our lives, and most of us have someone in our lives whom we claim to Love: our partners, families, friends, pets, etc. But this "Spiritual Love" of which I speak is altogether different. What I mean is, there is a connection we all share, and the genesis of this common bond is, indeed, Spiritual Love—it comes from God. Some of us are aware of this all-encompassing force, and live by it each and every day.

I say all this because acknowledging this common connection to other living beings can open your eyes to treating people, animals, and the environment with more respect. No, you may not simply "Love everyone" right away. But when you shift from dismissing or judging people to becoming more curious about the spiritual connection we all share, you take the pressure off of any uncomfortable encounters you may have with someone or something. And through this shift in perception, your stress level minimizes...your patience increases. You see yourself and God *in* other people. You grasp that we all come from the same place, and we really are one unified, complete family. So fast forward your growth and imagine if we all applied this knowledge into our everyday lives. Goodness, the possibilities...

Getting back to the early days of my spiritual exploration, I made sure I wasn't judging any of the content I was reading and/or hearing; I remained open to it all. I was a clean slate. And this process gave me the opportunity to truly absorb and understand all the possibilities of Spiritual Love, as defined by various authors, seminar leaders, and spiritual teachers. I learned we are all in various stages of spiritual development, and I felt I was taking an active role, participating in my life in new and exciting ways. I was consciously joyful, and went the extra mile for anyone, at any time. I was learning how to "walk the walk," so to speak.

I realized my newfound joy one chilly Thursday morning, when I didn't receive a "return smile" from a woman I passed while walking in a local park. Nevertheless, my internal reaction remained happy because, by smiling at the woman, I sent positive vibrations to the Universe and to her (whether she was aware of it or not). This is when I determined that, no matter what situation I faced in my life, I could focus inward and respond with heartfelt Love (as opposed to indignation or disdain). And I soon learned that only positive solutions emerge from this kind of conscious approach.

Anyway, as I implemented various teachings and reconditioning techniques into my daily practice, having a loving perspective made keeping to my spiritual Path much easier (and certainly more fun!). And this approach allowed for a seamless integration of the reconditioning process into my psyche and, most importantly, left less room for limiting thoughts or negative emotions.

The longer I practiced, the easier it all became. The epiphanies came more often. My outlook on life became more peaceful and fulfilling. These days, my own Layer Cake is in a constant state of evolution, because I continue to learn every day. In fact, one of my greatest joys in life is wondering what the new day holds? What will I learn? What magic will happen? How will I witness the Law of Attraction in action? And I now know that when I call to the Universe to claim what is abundantly mine, my desires will come, because I'm learning each day how to truly manifest them.

Here is my current daily practice:

I actually begin my "today" the night before. After I read in bed for bit, I give thanks for *at least* five awesome things that happened to me throughout that day. Simple or dramatic, it doesn't matter. I tend to consider the smaller things, though…those minute details. I find that when I appreciate something like running water, or a bird sitting on a fence post, more of the "good stuff" comes my way. So when I'm giving thanks before I go to sleep at night, I spend about

30 to 60 seconds giving *real* thanks for each event. Then I focus on the top experience of the day, fully giving gratitude for it, and why it enriches me with so much joy.

Once I've given my gratitude to the Universe, I close my eyes and visualize my dream life. This can last anywhere from three to 10 minutes, depending upon how tired I am. The intention behind this particular exercise is to reprogram my subconscious as I'm falling asleep, so I can manifest my desires more quickly. I attract that which I am, right?

So I make these two techniques (gratitude checklist and dream-life visualization) as fun and deliberate as I can. And once again, I'm "participating" with this process, not just sitting around in "spectating" mode, wondering why my desires aren't manifesting the way I want them to. These two foundational techniques also effectively set me up for a great night's sleep, putting me in a wonderful frame of mind when I awake in the morning.

When my internal alarm clock goes off around 6:10 a.m., a smile already occupies my face. Nothing has happened yet on this fresh new day, but I feel incredible even so! *What wonders will I experience today?!* I enthusiastically think to myself. And before my eyes even open, I'm giving gratitude for my awesome overall health, my cozy bed, the hot shower I'm about to experience, and the French press coffee I will soon be enjoying with Claudia.

I can't list all of the gratitude I give throughout each day, because it will take up too much space in this book! Suffice it to say, I speak "thank you" hundreds of times each day!

Once I get ready and leave the house, I drive to a park near my home, on the eastern shores of Lake Washington. On my short drive to the park, I know it's very important for me to focus on my wellbeing. So I keep my drive "sacred," as it were, not letting any of the day's up-and-coming challenges swirl around in my head—it's still "my time," after all! In other words, while fulfilling my morning practice of giving thanks, and being present, and getting ready, and driving to my favorite park, I don't allow the world's issues to penetrate my mind (and if they do, I use my Swerves or other techniques to keep myself present, grounded, and focused). And I make sure to smile, sometimes even laughing out loud in the car…"just because." While in the car, I normally listen to Wayne Dyer, classical music, or sports talk. Or sometimes I just enjoy silence and presence in the car—whatever puts me in the most peaceful and creative space.

Each morning, regardless of the time of year, the lake park is only visited by a handful of people. We all know each other by sight, and have occasionally shared a few words. I don't mind the early-morning conversations because, once again, I really enjoy all types of human interaction. There was a time, however, when I avoided talking with people as much as possible, because I didn't want their energy inside my bubble. I was too heavily concerned (or comfortable?) trying to be an expert on my own issues and problems, I guess. But thankfully, my daily practice has cured my need to avoid people!

But still, I prefer to use this quiet solo time as my opportunity to reflect, to be intentionally in the now, and to meditate. When I arrive at the park, I situate my car so I can see the embracing stillness of the lake. I then look out upon the expanses of grass and landscaping, while appreciating the large oak, maple, cedar, and fir trees. There is a bird sanctuary at the park as well, so the wildlife viewing is marvelous.

From there, I spend several minutes just being quiet and settling my mind. I do this so I can transition into the now where time is suspended. In this true state of observation, nothing exists other than peace. My body is totally relaxed. Yes, thoughts come and go, but nothing lingers; I always bring myself back to the now. I do this because I'm preparing myself for my morning meditation (thank you, Eckhart Tolle!).

This is my time when I focus on opening wide my channel and personal connection to God. I want to feel the abundant goodness and Love, which flows back and forth from my Creator to me… from me to my Creator. And it is during my morning meditation that answers come to me. No, I don't necessarily ask questions and/or wait for specific answers to come; I don't put parameters on my meditation. I just allow it to happen on its own, when it wants, in the way it wants. This way, I don't limit what naturally wants to flow to and through me. Sometimes "nothing" comes to me, and I'm simply left with the peace of quieting my mind. On rare occasions, however, monumental results can occur…like the day I "saw" my soul.

This was a moment that forever changed my life, and this momentous insight has allowed me to really focus *into* people, as opposed to just interacting with their masks. After the meditation when this insight occurred, I jumped up and immediately began pounding on my keyboard, writing like a madman! I found it quite difficult to articulate in words what that moment of divine insight meant to me. It all came through so simply, in layman's terms—yet is was much more challenging to translate onto paper what was communicated to me instantly in that life-changing moment. It's like standing at the edge of the Grand Canyon and experiencing its awe-inspiring grandeur, and then trying to convey it's awesomeness to someone over the phone. In the end, you are reduced to saying, "You'll see what I mean when you stand there for yourself!"

The following is the excerpt I journaled that very day, after having my astounding moment of insight!

The Joy of Liberation

I just had the best meditation of my life! It was a guided meditation by Deepak; it's part of an ongoing 21-day meditation series presented by Deepak and Oprah. This series is about joy and happiness. The central message of today's meditation was one of hope. I had missed a few days of my practice (which I don't like to do because I feel the effects it has on my life). But I always know that when I come back to it, I many times am surprised by the intensity I feel, the messages I get, or, in this case, the epiphany I just had! I can hardly believe it, but I discovered my soul today! I don't have the words to describe the feeling around this epiphany, but adjectives such as "boundless," "lightness," "purity," "joy," and, well… "of course I can do that, have that, be that" were/are extremely predominant.

I speak a lot of understanding things intellectually, but it's not until you truly "feel" something that it can have a real impact on you. Today, through meditation, my soul revealed itself to me! I was in "the gap" when I suddenly saw myself standing there. I've been practicing "living from my soul's perspective" for a long time. To me, that always meant living as spiritually as I could with a real focus on "walking the Path." And so far, it has been wonderful—paying huge dividends because all things in my life are now headed in the right direction.

So as I'm doing this guided meditation, I see myself standing there, when I suddenly envision myself as a softly glowing light in human form. My soul has round edges with no real definition…no finger or toes, no facial features. I'm now defining "myself" as "soul." Then I began to see myself. But while in the gap, as I'm feeling such immense joy trying to get my head around what's happening, I'm wondering whether I'm truly of human form…? Maybe I'm an emanating, glowing light about the size of a beach ball.

I haven't figured that out yet, but I can tell you that having discovered my true "self" today, I feel the field of infinite possibilities all around me. There is nothing that I can't do or be. I now feel a massive sense of accomplishment coming my way. I feel that I have so much to offer mankind and all living things.

I am bursting at the seams with the possibilities of each moment that I am breathing into now. What gloriousness will happen today!?

I am now truly in alignment with my desires!

It's difficult for me to interpret the impact of that moment into the written word for you here. It was a very special moment for me. I hope to soon have similar experiences. After reflecting on what happened that day, I can tell you it was only through the practice of opening my mind that I was able to reach that depth of awareness.

If you and I are ever blessed to speak in person, please ask me about this. The passion that pours from me whenever I recant that moment is quite evident and contagious. You can probably see how that life-changing instant was responsible for galvanizing my dharma.

So onward we forge!

When my morning meditation is complete (we're back at the lake again now), I sit in utter repose for about five minutes, totally still, thinking of nothing. Glorious! This early-morning practice is the foundation of a healthy day for me. It sets me up to remain in a solid and loving state, regardless of what the day may bring. This practice is critical in keeping me to my Path.

After 20 to 40 minutes in the park, I then head to my office, where I begin my workday by reading and writing. First I review my list of desires, visualizing them as if I'm already living them. Then I set my intentions for the day: "As I go through my day, I will live with Love and joy in my heart. I will give whatever I can to whoever needs me, without sacrificing the quality of my own wellbeing. I will work efficiently all day in order to maximize my time. I will keep my eyes and heart open to learning and to new opportunities, which will better my life and the lives of those around me."

Next, I check my phone "mantra events" (think back to "Belief Eight"), so I can stay inspired and acutely aware of "participating" throughout the day. The rest of the day I propagate thoughts of allowing, gratitude, Love, patience, non-judgment, and giving. I also focus on performing all of my tasks with joy, so I can earn a good living. I find no room for complaint, resentment, jealousy, regret, worry, or anger. In fact, I find it difficult to even say those words. I am steadfastly aware that these negative emotions do nothing more than bring disease to me. And so I rest patiently in Love, as I attract that which I am.

On the weekends, Claudia and I will spend an hour or so watching spiritual programming. Many interesting ideas and conversations come about, as we pop in a new DVD, while sipping coffee and noshing on fruit, cheese and bread...and butter. It's a joy to have someone in my life who is as willing and interested in living a spiritual life as I am. Even though Claudia and I each follow our own Path, there is an unspoken woven growth we are experiencing together.

I've been practicing like this for years, and I don't have the words to tell you how incredibly joyful I feel. I look back at my life prior to beginning my spiritual practice and realize how far I've come. I think what I've garnered most from my practice is the innate knowing that everything is just great, and something special is always on its way. The negative situations which used to grab and hold onto me simply don't exist anymore. And the repetitive cycles of worried thinking that typically filled my days have all but vanished—even better, they have been replaced with cool possibilities, a thriving curiosity, and an abundance of creativity. Yes, this has been my experience thus far, and I look forward to hearing about *your* experience, your Path, and your conscious evolution.

I'm certainly not perfect, but I do feel like my life has been cleansed. So for those of you who think you cannot do this, or feel you do not have the time, I understand. It can seem discouraging if you compare where I am today, with where you are right now. But just start small...with a deep breath. Embarking on a lifelong spiritual journey with positive intent is a wonderful opportunity to undergo. So remember, one moment at a time.

I once stood where you do today—and I promise you, it did not take immense strength to get to where I am now. You can do this! Yes, you, too, will shepherd in a new existence for yourself. Simply apply slight shifts throughout your day, and before you know it you'll be well on your way. Freedom is your birthright; it is yours to be had. You are on your way to learning how to manage your thought patterns, while allowing your soul to unfurl. So learn to leverage your mind's vast ability to think all things positive.

I've learned so much over the years about myself, God, and the spiritual connection we all share. And yes, there are some people out there who've had intense, instantaneous awakenings that vaulted them straight to enlightenment, with no need for any sort of reconditioning process. In an instant, they simply "got it," and that was it! And you know, that is awesome! But for the rest of us, the Path toward God-realization is a moment-by-moment endeavor. So understand that, for most of us, this process does take time. But when you allow joy to permeate, it is not difficult. It is the coolest feeling to steadfastly take the first step or two along your Path, making your declaration, only to wake up a few months later feeling differently…feeling better! And as you Keep to Your Spiritual Path, those moments never stop happening.

Now it's time to take another emotional inventory!

Honestly, I want to know how far you've come since first starting this book. Is it helping you? Were you ready for it when you first picked it up?

The purpose of *this* emotional inventory is to see how you stack up…right now! But this time I've slightly modified the questions with the expectation that, by now, you have read and applied some of this book's empowering philosophies to your life:

- Am I dealing with fewer surface issues?
- Is it easier to address the deeper issues of my life?
- Am I embracing change?
- Am I feeling good most of the time?
- Do I have healthier cyclical thoughts each day?
- What new thoughts do I have?
- How much has my stress level reduced?
- What are the most important things in my life?
- How has joy impacted my life?
- Which tools have I implemented to improve my emotional state each moment?
- How much better do I feel today?
- Which new life change is my favorite?

- What's the best part about change?
- Which books will I read this month?
- How much has implementing a flexible mindset helped me in my life?
- How has my emotional honesty improved my productivity?
- YES! Now!
- YES! Me!
- YES! I love myself!

Eventually, all of these "questions" will morph into "statements" (they may even become mantras you program into your phone!). You have begun a new chapter in your life, and now you are ready for anything. Remember, your time is *now!* Your healthy wellbeing is increasing in each moment, as is the quality of your life experience. Now pass it forward!

So what has Fresh Beliefs taught you?

In Belief One, we invest in the beauty of your Why? because it is your ultimate motivator. It is the reason you choose to walk a spiritual Path. In order to spark your shift to all things abundant, I give you the important step of Belief Two. Here you change your tone in the messages you deliver to people while simultaneously improving your underlying aura. It feels so nice to speak in positive terms! Uplifted by good feelings you are challenged in Belief Three to rid yourself of fear. We lift the veil of the ego in order to eliminate it early in the process. Otherwise it will stunt or totally inhibit your spiritual growth. As fear is minimized, the light pours in. Flooded by this light, your spark grows, putting you in position to prepare yourself for your journey with the help of Belief Four. Visualizing your Path and understanding how you will travel it, gives you the sense of how you will garner spiritual information, which you will learn in Belief Five through the exciting gift of curiosity.

During your exploration, your constant reminder of balance, beauty, peace and abundance is given to you by the laws of Nature in Belief Six. Inspired by Nature's grandeur, Belief Seven introduces metaphorical Bricks for your Path so that your new life will have solid footing. Belief Eight provides moment-to-moment, second nature principles that can take you to the highest levels of enlightenment as your practice distills into your new way of life as taught in Belief Nine. Implement Fresh Beliefs consistently over time and you truly will realize your dreams. What does Belief Ten mean to you? Develop and own your practice while asking for nothing in return. Make serving your fellow man, the animals and the planet your primary focus.

One last question: In what ways do you feel differently regarding your overall approach to life? And what has made the difference? Whatever it is, keep at it... Keep to Your Path. It gets better and easier every day!

The primary vision in my life now is God; I feel God is our Originator. We all stem from God. I believe God is energy, and is in everything we experience. I see God all around me, in all shapes and colors. I also see God as a vibrant globe of infinite, unconditional Love. And I see each one of us as beams connected to Him, much like the sun's rays emanating in all directions. Since we are all united with this ultimate abundance, this means that we, too, all have unlimited abundance within us.

I feel the connection we have with God ebbs and flows in different degrees, depending on the conscious awareness we have of our existence, and how in touch with God we are relative to each moment. Where we may feel "dis-connected" from God, we never truly are. The connection may be stretched thin and seemingly holding on by a thread at times, but it never snaps—never! Yes, sometimes the abundant flow of God's energy seems stagnant or slowed but, in reality, it is always there, working for us, not against us.

My personal goal is to maintain a healthy, open flow with God, keeping the pipeline free of joy-pilfering debris, so the Universe's abundance can circulate through me unencumbered—and to practice Love, giving, and non-judgment by ultimately stringing together one glorious moment to the next. Lace together beautiful moments, emanate joy, and happiness will follow.

Your spiritual journey will now be one of participation, joy, and peace. You will read, study, apply, and reap the abundant fruit, which is waiting to flow to you. Remember to grow at your own pace, and know that your enthusiasm for growth will help in propelling you forward. Just remember to keep your awareness sharp and "switched on" at all times. And when you feel your thoughts starting to churn, just keep bringing yourself back to the now; live in the moment!

There will come times on your journey when you believe you are "finished." In that moment, look to the sky for a few seconds with a smile on your face…then look within for God. Know the feeling of "being finished" is actually the *beginning* of something new and beautiful. Rejoice in the magnificence of the next step.

Fair warning: Be aware that too much enthusiasm along your Path may keep you from the most important goal of "Being." In other words, don't get so caught up in the research, learning, and visualizations you're applying that you forget to slow down and allow yourself to "just be."

> Though my piety is ever-present
> I sometimes forget
> It is through stillness
> My awakenings beget
> —STK

The most fulfilling aspect of a consistent, healthy practice is reveling in the fruit of intentionally manifesting my desires. I have condensed all that I've learned into daily activities that focus on Love, giving and applying principles that work for me. Today, Claudia and I are living heaven on Earth. You, too, can experience the bounty of our abundant Universe by allowing yourself to become totally vulnerable to the spiritual process. It is from your trust in the beauty of the unknown that your ultimate desire for peace and sanctuary will germinate.

You are a shepherd!

Again, give of yourself to mankind, the animals, and the

environment. There is a global shift happening right now. We are all beginning to hold hands in a unified understanding, focusing on harmony and Love. Peace is the only way. And believe it or not, you can help to accelerate this process by just Being…allowing your tolerance to spread to those you touch.

As you continue to benefit from your steady Spiritual practice, someone may say to you, "What are you doing differently? You seem to be in such a good place!" And you might respond with, "Well, I've learned to become more aware of how I feel. I've been applying some new ideas, and doing a lot of reading and self-reflection. This has really kept me on track, and I feel much better because of it." You may also hear from someone, "I'm in such a bad place. What should I do?" This is your opportunity to give back to another soul by saying, "Start telling a new story, give something special every day, and begin expressing gratitude for everything you have in your life right now. This will teach you to be aware of how you feel about things. That way, you can bring yourself back to feeling good more quickly. Stick to it for a month, and watch your life begin to shift."

Some people may even be ready to hear you talk about moving away from fear by detaching from negative emotions. Or perhaps you can encourage them to focus on the positive aspects that life has to offer. Take whatever you learn here, and from the other sources you choose to study, and cast your magic dust upon every person and animal with whom you come in contact.

Remember, Love is always the answer, and it will solve all of your issues. Love creates the space with which you can move through a challenging moment in complete peace. The magic tonic you seek is Love. Try it. It works!

Full Circle: Can it be we all cycle through perpetual, physical lifetimes, discovering the deeper meaning of life during each succession? And if this is true, each time we die in a physical life, we individually reunite with God, and are blissfully reminded of our indescribable Love, abundance, and potential. Then we, once again, re-enter the physical realm to learn new lessons and to broadcast our beliefs to others. Ultimately, when we as a collective of souls simultaneously reach a moment of conscious spiritual unity, we will all return home to God.

As I've undergone the wonderful journey of continued self-discovery during the writing of this book, I find myself, once again, asking the question: What is spirituality? This time, my response is much simpler:

For me, spirituality is the way home.

Reference Books

Choose Yourself – James Altucher
The Power of No – James and Claudia Altucher
The Motivation Manifesto – Brendon Burchard
The Magic – Rhonda Byrne
The Hero – Rhonda Byrne
The Seven Spiritual Laws of Success – Dr. Deepak Chopra
Change Your Thoughts, Change Your Life – Dr. Wayne Dyer
Getting in the Gap – Dr. Wayne Dyer
In Beauty May I Walk – Helen Exley
E2 – Pam Grout
The Holy Bible
You Can Heal Your Life – Louise Hay
Ask and It Is Given – Esther and Jerry Hicks
The Power of Deliberate Intent – Esther and Jerry Hicks
Daily Calm – National Geographic
The Tapping Solution – Nick Ortner
The Mastery of Love – don Miguel Ruiz
The Four Agreements - don Miguel Ruiz
A Course in Miracles – Helen Schucman and William Thetford
The Power of Now – Eckhart Tolle
A New Earth - Eckart Tolle

About the Author

Spencer T. King's expertise is rooted in a lifetime of focus on peaceful thought. With over 30 years of study in spirituality, diverse cultures, as well as the natural environment, his *Fresh Beliefs* Principles embolden people to discover their life's purpose by keeping to a chosen spiritual Path. A period of deep self-reflection following a dark saga in Spencer's life inspired him to develop *Fresh Beliefs*, which gave him the bearings he needed to find his way and, ultimately, his life's purpose. Spencer is known for his natural charisma, down-to-earth nature, and ability to relate to individuals from all walks of life. Spencer now devotes his time to serving others who wish to tailor his *Fresh Beliefs* approach into their own lives. An entrepreneur and international traveler, Spencer lives in Kirkland, Washington. For more information, go to http://spencertking.com.

Allow your soul to emerge,
BLOOM & live !
Pg xx..   - Self discovery
                Hand in hand w/
                God !

              - True passion =
                Your Destiny .

              - Receive All the
                God has for you.

   Thank you   I am abundantly
   Lord !   Blessed.

Seed

Printed in the United States
By Bookmasters